BALLET ART

From the Renaissance to the Present

by Mary Clarke and Clement Crisp

79-07108

Clarkson N. Potter, Inc./Publishers NEW YORK

DISTRIBUTED BY CROWN PUBLISHERS, INC.

For Nadia Nerina
a ballerina who loves art

First published in the U.S.A. in 1978 by
Clarkson N. Potter Inc.
One Park Avenue, New York, N.Y. 10016

Produced by Ash & Grant Limited
120B Pentonville Road, London N1 9JB

Printed by Balding + Mansell Limited
Wisbech, Cambridgeshire

Library of Congress Cataloging in Publication Data

Clarke, Mary 1923–
Ballet Art
1. Ballet in Art   2. Art. I. Crisp, Clement II. Title.
N8217 .B35C55 1978   704.94'9'7928   78–7195
ISBN 0 517 53454 1
ISBN 0 517 53455 X pbk.

BALLET
ART

CONTENTS

INTRODUCTION

Maria Medina Viganò as
Terpsichore

*It is the movement of people which consoles us; if the
leaves on the trees did not move, how sad the trees would
be, and so should we.*

Edgar Degas

Ever since man learned to make graphic representations of the
world that surrounded him he has sought to capture on an
immobile surface the movement he observed. The earliest
surviving cave paintings show this in their portrayal of hunting or
of tribal activity. It is a commonplace that in the art of the ancient
world we find depicted ritual and celebration in which dance is a
crucial factor. The purpose of this book, however, is to offer some
insights into the most sophisticated and stylised form of dancing
that has been devised by Western civilisation. This is the classic
academic dance – the 'Ballet' of today's vocabulary. It is an art
which has its most evident origins in the court life of the
Renaissance, where dance was an essential part of the education of
the aristocracy. The festivities of the Renaissance were all aspects
of the elaborate machinery of state whose aim was the glorification
of the prince and of the idea of monarchy. The court provided the
setting; the courtiers provided both performers and audience.

In displays of every kind, in tournaments, in explosions of
fireworks (the artist Bernardo Buontalenti was nicknamed *delle
Girandole* – 'of the fireworks' – because he devised, among other
and more important decorative matters, firework displays for the
Medici festivities in Florence), in water pageants, in danced
intermezzi introduced into plays, in masquerades and in horse
ballets, as well as in the court ballets in which the monarch and his
nobles participated, we can trace a variety of elements which were
eventually to contribute to the emergence of 'Ballet' as a theatrical
form in the latter part of the seventeenth century. At this moment,
when the last of the noble amateurs – Louis XIV – had ceased to
perform, there came an important divide in the history of dancing.
The advent of professional training provided the foundation for
the development of ballet in the theatre; for the amateurs there
remained the various and rich forms of social dance.

The correspondence between ballet and its audience can be
identified in differing degrees through the iconography of artists
of all kinds who recorded it. Sometimes the most pertinent and

revealing view of an epoch may be found in caricature, in which the sharp eye of satire penetrates layers of pretence to capture some essential fact – as in certain Russian caricatures at the end of the nineteenth century. These saw through the elaborate paraphernalia of the ballerina as virtuoso and goddess to the dancer as a charmer decked with jewels.

More usually the representations of dancers were simply portraits, celebrating their beauty and charm as human beings rather than their identity as performing artists: Gainsborough's painting of Giovanna Baccelli is a case in point. Occasionally a major artist became deeply involved with the dancer as athlete, as the figure of stretched muscles and aching back – the often contorted and unexpected shape to be seen in a fleeting moment in class. Such was Degas. His multitudinous studies of dancers remain the supreme commentary upon the dancer as paradigm and symbol of movement.

Between the poles of caricature and great painting there lies an extraordinary range of representation of ballet. We have been concerned wherever possible with paintings, sculptures, drawings and engravings which capture performance rather than the static performer. Nevertheless, such curiosities as an eighteenth-century paper doll, a nineteenth-century soap wrapper featuring Marie Taglioni, the greatest divinity of the Romantic era, and twentieth-century postage stamps all suggest odd ways in which ballet has impinged upon society. The relationship of ballet to the society which gave it birth and nutured it can be inferred from the ways in which it was represented to the public of its time. How dancers were dressed tells us not only about the possibilities of their technique but also of their sexual identity: we have but to consider the elaborate skirts of the ballerina in the middle of the eighteenth century to understand how restricted was both her dancing and her role in society. Within fifty years the draperies of the Neoclassic period show how the *ancien régime* had given way to a very different political and social milieu. The etherealisation of the ballerina in the Romantic period, when lithographs reveal her poised like a wisp of mist in the night air, tells how ballet itself had changed in the public imagination and had become an art of escape, of fugitive images and impossible love. The steady decline – with a few very honourable exceptions – in the representation of dancing in the twentieth century reflects not a decline in the importance of ballet but the arrival of the camera as the ideal medium for capturing movement. The work of such exceptional camera artists as Baron de Meyer at the beginning of the century, and Anthony Crickmay today, can take us so near the very heart of performance that the painter or sculptor has far less incentive to treat of ballet.

Émile-Antoine Bourdelle, *Nijinsky as Harlequin in 'Le Carnaval'*

RENAISSANCE SPECTACLE

Nothing is so necessary to men as dancing.

Molière *Le Bourgeois Gentilhomme*

The aristocratic view of the human body which lies at the root of the training in the classic academic dance is attributable to the princely origins of ballet itself in the entertainments of the Renaissance. The court spectacles which developed in Italy in the fifteenth century, and which spread from there throughout Europe, were designed to glorify the image of the prince as ruler. By every form of display, from jousts to banquets, the *persona* of the ruler was subject to an aggrandisement which was intended to dazzle and impress courtiers and public. The celebrations of dynastic marriages, of triumphal entries, of alliances, were seen as metaphors of royal power and they served to stress the importance of the central figure in the eyes of other rulers as well as of the general populace. The festivities served also to propagate the idea of the quasi-divine nature of the prince.

Transitory though these spectacles were, they employed many of the finest artists available, whose gifts were best rewarded in the service of the prince: Tintoretto and Veronese, Holbein, Leonardo and Inigo Jones were all concerned at one time or another with providing decorative material for royal progresses. The development of the theatre in western Europe, following the rediscovery of Vitruvius' principles of the classic stage, owes much to the intermezzi and ballets that were the ephemeral celebrations of some royal event.

The festivals of the Medici in Florence made use for sixty years of the work of Buontalenti. The Florentine Catherine de'Medici, as Queen of France, provided a vital impulse to the expansion of court festivities in Paris and throughout France. Two of the most significant court ballets – the *Ballet des Polonais* of 1573 and the *Ballet Comique de la Reine* of 1581 – were to establish a tradition in France of *ballet de cour* which was to reach its apogee under Louis XIV and then lead on to the establishment of the professional ballet in 1670.

The form of the emergent court ballet in France was a combination of speech and declamation, music and song, machines (whereby divinities might descend among the mortals) and social dance. The vocabulary of movement used was quite simply that of the court dances of the period; the interest lay in the

1 Jacques Patin, Frontispiece to *Le Ballet Comique de la Reine*. Etching, 1582. *Le Ballet Comique de la Reine*, a five-hour entertainment, is celebrated in dance history as being the first ballet for which a published libretto is generally known. Patin, who was *peintre du Roi*, decorated this dramatic spectacle and his etching gives a fair indication of the scene in the Grand Salle de Bourbon in the Louvre in September 1581. This opening scene shows a courtier addressing the Royal party. The audience viewed the progress of the piece, an allegory about the freeing of enslaved man by royal power, from tiered seats on either side of the hall.

2 Pellegrino Tibaldi, *A Dancing Genius*. Pen and wash.

patterning and pulse of the steps rather than in any complexity of individual footwork. These entertainments paid obvious tribute to their presiding royal genius by being performed to 'the presence'. The royal party was to be found in a central and sometimes raised location. To them the entire entertainment was directed; the attendant courtiers would watch in tiered and serried ranks around the main performance area in a palace hall, or deferentially fanned out around the presence of the monarch.

The fact that the monarch and his courtiers performed suggests something of the importance attributed to these dance spectacles. Behind the most elaborate of these there often lay a very clear political message. The *Ballet des Polonais* was presented expressly to consolidate the position of the Duc d'Anjou, third son of Catherine de'Medici, as newly elected King of Poland. The Polish Ambassadors, arrived in Paris, were presented with this entertainment in which ladies of Catherine's household appeared on a silver-gilt rock, each representing one of the French regions and each paying tribute in verse to Henri d'Anjou. Descending from the rock, the ladies moved through carefully ordered patterns of movement devised by Belgioioso, Catherine's Italian dancing master. It was Belgioioso, whose name was adapted for the French to Beaujoyeulx, who was to devise the greatest of these early court ballets, the *Ballet Comique de la Reine*. This five-hour spectacle was presented as part of a sequence of festivities lasting two weeks which celebrated the marriage of the King of France's favourite, the Duc de Joyeuse, to the King's sister-in-law, Marguerite of Lorraine. So important was this *Ballet Comique* felt to be in suggesting the monarch's supremacy at a time of political unrest that a careful description was printed and circulated round the major royal houses of Europe. It survives as the most fascinating and complete record of an early French court spectacle.

The representations of court entertainments of every kind give us an invaluable insight into the attitudes as well as the appearance of Renaissance magnificences. Design drawings, official records of the wide range of royal entertainments, indicate how prodigal was the expenditure and no less extreme the ingenuity with which these affairs were presented. The Valois tapestries provide some indication of what was felt to be a most important enterprise. The illustrations to the *Ballet Comique de la Reine*; the series of design paintings by Buontalenti; the engravings by Cantagallina after Parigi of Florentine intermezzi; Callot's closely detailed observation of princely entertainments; indeed, the whole vast corpus of records of royal entertainments, all tell of the way in which public imagination was caught and stimulated.

The culminating days of court ballet came with Louis XIV of France. It is worth recording that his title of *Le Roi Soleil* came to him initially from his appearance as the Sun in the *Ballet Royal de la Nuit* in 1653. By now the *ballet de cour* was at its most complex: a series of entries upon a theme might serve merely to amuse an audience, but sometimes political motivation was retained. So it was in the *Ballet Royal de la Nuit*, where the young king's unassailable power and the blaze of his majesty were symbolised in his role as the Sun itself.

In this greatest age of the arts in France, the King's love of dancing and his participation in all forms of court display inspired remarkable illustrations of royal entertainments. In June 1662 a carrousel (a horse ballet) was staged in Paris – hence today's Place du Carrousel – to celebrate the birth of the Dauphin. The engraver Chauveau's record of this event is one of the most splendid annals of the period. Two years later, a series of entertainments in the grounds of the Palace of Versailles were staged under the title *Les Plaisirs de l'Ile Enchantée*, when for three days the court enjoyed comedies, ballets, banquets and equestrian displays, all dutifully fixed for posterity by Israel Silvestre. The portrayal of these opulent displays, and of the no less splendid entertainments with which the Habsburg court sought to make Vienna a rival to Versailles, indicates the imaginative fantasy as well as the vast extravagance with which the last years of the court ballets were illuminated.

The artist's view of these events – Küsel's engravings of Burnacini's designs for *Il Pomo d'Oro* in Vienna in 1668, Chauveau's and Silvestre's records of the work of the designers Gissey and Vigarani at Versailles – capture all that is best and most entrancing. They are, of course, in many ways idealised as views of performance. Nevertheless, contemporary descriptions indicate that huge sums were to be spent on the caparisoning of horse and rider in the carrousels, and immense ingenuity went into the creation of the world of fantastic illusion in the Baroque theatre exemplified by Burnacini. There were no fewer than twenty-one scene changes in *Il Pomo d'Oro*, each as prodigious as the last. Because these displays were intended to dazzle and excite, and to reiterate to the public the theme of royal power, iconography of the period offers precious testimony to a monarch's aspirations, to his way of life.

At the end of the 1660s Louis XIV gave up his participation in court ballets. This decision has been variously ascribed to his increasing portliness, but whatever the reason, it is significant that at this time the production of ballet passed into the hands of professionals. More especially there emerged the form of the opera-ballet staged at the Académie Royale de Musique in Paris under the absolute command of Jean-Baptiste Lully. Lully, sometime a dancer and later violinist to the King, obtained the royal *privilège* which enabled him alone to present lyric works. With the King's ballet master, Pierre Beauchamps, he codified the entertainment of opera-ballet into a combination of sung scenes interspersed with danced interludes. Lully's successors developed and extended the form of the opera-ballet without radically altering it. The emergence of a dance school at the Académie Royale de Musique was in due time to guarantee a supply of well trained dancers, and the later development of ballet as an art on its own drew upon the dance traditions of both France and Italy.

3 Henri Gissey, Costume for a male dancer representing a ship. This design comes from a book of costume drawings.

4 Carrousel in the Place Royale, Paris

4 Anonymous German engraving of the Carrousel given in April 1612 in the Place Royale, Paris. The medieval tradition of knightly jousting gradually became refined into a decorative display of horsemanship known as a Carrousel. Elaborated into a processional form, calling upon all the arts of designers to produce decorated cars and fantasy of costuming for horse as well as rider, the Carrousel, like other court entertainments, was used to proclaim the splendour of the monarchy. In 1612 the cementing of an alliance between France and Spain was marked by the double betrothal of Louis XIII to Anne of Austria, Infanta of Spain, and of Philip, Prince of the Asturias, heir to the Spanish throne, to Elisabeth of France. This engraving provides a magnificent, if slightly innocent, record of the various cars which joined the quadrilles of horsemen, and it shows the culminating effect of the firework display in which royal emblems (and later, royal portraits) blazed out.

5 Jacques Callot after Giulio Parigi, *La Guerra de Bellezza*. Engraving, 1616. The arrival of the Prince

of Urbino in Florence as bridegroom to Claudia de' Medici was celebrated with much pomp, culminating in the tremendous public spectacle of a horse ballet on the Piazza Santa Croce. In this, as in the *ballet de cour*, part of the interest lay in what we would now describe as floor patterns. Complication of step mattered not at all. Like the courtier, whose vocabulary of movement was limited to the steps of the social dance of his time, the horse and its rider had but a limited range of trotting or galloping steps. For the audience the excitement lay in fantasy of costuming, in elaboration of symbolism and allegory, and in the fascination of the patterns created. Callot's magnificent engraving catches all the popular excitement (it was reported that more than 25,000 spectators viewed the ballet from the grandstands, or from roof tops) of this display.

6 Bonnart, *Monsieur Ballon*. Engraving. Jean Ballon was a principal dancer at the Paris Opéra at the beginning of the eighteenth century. He was famous for the buoyant quality in his dancing and he enjoyed the patronage of the King.

5 Jacques Callott after Giulio Parigi, *La Guerra de Bellezza*

6 Bonnart, *Monsieur Ballon*

7 Aveline after Giacomo Torelli, *Les Noces de Pélée et de Thétis*

7 Aveline after Giacomo Torelli, Scene from *Les Noces de Pélée et de Thétis*. Engraving. Torelli was one of the greatest designers of the mid-seventeenth century, celebrated for his brilliance in the use of stage machinery. The emergence of a framed, proscenium stage encouraged Torelli during his early years in Venice in experiments which were to create a remarkably fluid stage area. Summoned to France in 1645 to work for Anne of Austria, Torelli was one of the founders of the French 'theatre of machines'. In this engraving, of one of the most important ballets of the early years of Louis XIV's reign (in which the King took the role of Apollo in the first scene), Torelli's architectural skill and feeling for perspective is evident. The ballet was first staged in the Salle du Palais Bourbon in Paris in 1654. The engraving was made slightly later. As records of performance such prints served to disseminate through Europe the ideas of splendour and opulence associated with the French court theatre.

8 Jacques Callot after Giulio Parigi, View of the first intermezzo in *La Liberazione di Tireno e d'Arnea*. Etching. Callot's etchings are among the most intriguing views we have of court entertainments of the early seventeenth century, in both France and Italy. His own sense of the dramatic brings great immediacy to his presentation of these spectacles. *La Liberazione* was a *veglia*, or vigil, in which the interpolated dance scenes were considered particularly remarkable. This illustration shows the inside of the Teatro Medici, designed by Buontalenti, in the Uffizi Palace. It depicts the first intermezzo, in which a volcano is erupting above the body of a giant. The performance was given in honour of the marriage of the Duke of Mantua to Catherine de' Medici in February 1617. Callot indicates the way in which the stage performance was brought into the auditorium and, as in the *ballet de cour*, the final *grand ballet* united performers and audience.

8 Jacques Callot after Giulio Parigi, *La Liberazione di Tireno e d' Arnea*

9 Matthaus Küsel after Lodovico Burnacini, *Il Pomo d'Oro*

9 Matthaus Küsel after Lodovico Burnacini, *Il Pomo d'Oro*. Engraving. The political rivalry between France and Austria was reflected in the elaboration of spectacle in Versailles and Vienna. Greatest and most extravagant of the Viennese stagings at the end of the seventeenth century was the amazing production given of Antonio Cesti's opera *Il Pomo d'Oro*, with its danced interludes. It was presented in 1667 as the culmination of the marriage celebrations between the Emperor Leopold I and the Infanta Margareta Theresa. Burnacini, pre-eminent stage designer of his time, achieved in this production the consummation of high Baroque design. The theme of the Judgement of Paris was an excuse for a virtuoso presentation whose twenty-one scenes piled stage miracle upon stage miracle. The brilliance of mechanics in Baroque theatrecraft encouraged a designer like Burnacini to dazzle his audience, very necessarily, with scenes which reflected the magnificence of his royal master, while also flattering royal pretensions to quasi-divinity. The engraving shows an apotheosis which suggests the martial triumphs to be associated with Leopold I.

10 *Mademoiselle Subligny dancing at the Paris Opéra*. Engraving, c. 1700. Marie Subligny was a principal dancer at the Paris Opéra, succeeding in this position Mademoiselle Lafontaine, one of the first four professional female dancers. Subligny was noted for the grace and nobility of her style, qualities which marked the French manner of dancing at this time

and remained its distinguishing characteristic during the eighteenth century. The image presented in this engraving is entirely just: stage dress was at this time a heightened form of court dress. In this it reflected the attitudes of the *ballet de cour*, wherein the noble amateur wore his best for even an unimportant role.

11 *Le Ballet de la Délivrance de Renaud*. Wood engraving from the libretto. During the early years of the reign of Louis XIII a series of remarkably extravagant court ballets were staged under the influence of the King's favourite, the Duc de Luynes. Highly dramatic, these lavish enterprises also served a political purpose: the production of *Renaud* was intended to indicate that the King was asserting his authority instead of allowing his mother, Marie de' Medici, to direct affairs of state. The theme of the ballet came from that fruitful source of dramatic ideas, Tasso's *Gerusalemme Liberata*, and was concerned with the freeing of Renaud from the enchantments of the sorceress Armida. In the scene illustrated, Armida has summoned up her demons and they appear first in the form of crayfish, turtles and snails. Throwing off these disguises, they are next seen as old women. This wood engraving from the account of the ballet published at the time of its first performance was meant to suggest to a larger public the theme rather than the actuality of the performance.

10 *Mademoiselle Subligny dancing at the Paris Opéra*

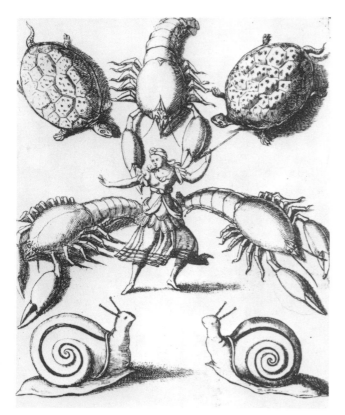

11 *Le Ballet de la Délivrance de Renaud*

Pages 18–19

12 *The Valois tapestries: the reception of the Polish ambassadors.* c. 1580. Among the most remarkable testimonies to the court life and the political ambitions of the House of Valois are the eight tapestries woven in Brussels which feature Catherine de' Medici and her sons who were successively kings of France. Though each tapestry ostensibly relates to a single event, collectively they represent a summation of the use of spectacle for propaganda purposes. In one tapestry we are shown the reception in 1573 of the Polish ambassadors who had come to France to invite Catherine de' Medici's third son, Henri d'Anjou, to rule Poland. The occasion was celebrated by a 'ballet' on August 19 in the Palace of the Tuileries. The panoramic view of court behaviour is here transferred to the open air so that the formal gardens may be admired; the style of court dancing is excellently depicted in the foreground figures who are seen in the general dance that habitually ended a court ballet, while the figure of Catherine is the focal point of the whole design, indicating her political importance.

13 Bernardo Buontalenti, Designs for the costumes of two female dancers. For nearly sixty years Bernardo Buontalenti acted as a designer and master of theatrical crafts for the Medici in Florence. These costumes indicate both the beauty and complexity of design and the freedom which they yet allowed for movement. They were also to be 'read' by the public as illustrating certain moral or physical qualities.

14 Herman van der Most (attrib.), *Ball at the court of Henri III*. The occasion of the marriage in 1581 of the King's favourite Anne, Duc de Joyeuse, to Marguerite of Lorraine, sister of Queen Louise, was celebrated by one of the greatest series of festivities in France in the sixteenth century. These are known as the Joyeuse 'Magnificences' and they lasted for two weeks, during which time a different entertainment was given on each day. The most celebrated of these was the *Ballet Comique de la Reine* (plate 1). The political motivation behind these 'Magnificences' lay in the profound unease in religious matters then affecting France: the question was not of conciliating the Reformed Church as represented by the Huguenots, but of pacifying the ultra-Catholic 'league'. This Counter-Reformation movement centred on the House of Lorraine and besides marrying into that House, King Henri – shown at the extreme left, near dowager Queen Catherine – sought to strengthen his connection by doing great honour to his favourite, the Duc of Joyeuse, who was also allying himself with the House of Lorraine. The Joyeuse 'Magnificences' were thus a studied political action.

12 *The Valois tapestries: The reception of the Polish Ambassadors*

13 Bernardo Buontalenti, Costumes for two dancers.

15 *Il Carnevale Languente.* 1647. Count Filippo d'Aglié was a nobleman turned theatrical producer. He was responsible during a period of three decades for ballet productions at the Court of Savoy. Here, in court theatres and also in princely castles, d'Aglié was master of design, production and machines, and sometimes librettist and musician for court entertainments. These excited great popular acclaim and are a most interesting development of the *ballet de cour* in Italy. Our illustration from the entertainment staged for the Duchess of Savoy, sister of Louis XIII of France, shows Count Giorgio di Mombasilio dancing the part of the melancholic earthy humour.

14 Herman van der Most (attrib.), *Ball at The Court of Henri III*

15 *Il Carnevale Languente*

BALLET INTO
THE THEATRE

A ballet is a picture, or rather a series of pictures connected one with the other by the plot which provides the theme of the ballet; the stage is, as it were, the canvas on which the composer expresses his ideas; the choice of the music, scenery and costumes are his colours; the composer is the painter.

Jean-Georges Noverre

The advent of professional dancers brought the rise of the star performer who triumphed through skill rather than through social position, as had happened in the *ballet de cour*. But social dress remained the basic shape of theatrical costume, and men's clothes allowed for more freedom of movement than did the long and heavily draped skirts of women performers. It was thus inevitable that throughout the century the male dancer was to be the dominant figure technically, and the few main traditions of eighteenth-century theatrical dance are those associated with men. The greatest figure of the early years of the century was Louis Dupré, Le Grand Dupré, the first *danseur noble* to earn that illustrious soubriquet, *Le Dieu de la danse*. His pupil Gaetano Vestris was Italian born but made his name in France and succeeded Dupré as a principal of the Paris Opéra where he was no less celebrated as a master of the *style noble*, considered the highest pinnacle of the art of dancing. Auguste Vestris, his son by his mistress the ballerina Marie Allard, followed him as the foremost male star in Europe, albeit his style was the more brilliant but less grand *demi-caractère*.

With these three dancers we bridge the entire history of dancing, from the opera-ballet to the dawn of the Romantic movement and that moment when the ballerina finally comes into her own. Even so, the female dancer was early to make her mark in the theatre. The first professional female dancers had been seen in 1681, but, like their immediate successors, their dancing was constricted by the conventions of dress which required them to appear in elaborated versions of court clothing. Yet female vanity being what it is, the first notable development in the costume of the *danseuse* came when Marie Camargo shortened her skirts to just above the ankles so that the public might admire her feet twinkling in an *entrechat*. For more serious artistic reasons her contemporary

16 Nicolas Lancret, *Le Moulinet devant la Charmille*. This enchanting picture is a study of dancing as part of a *fête galante*. The *Moulinet* of the title is the figure formed by the four dancers whose hands are crossed. The entire scene speaks of untrammelled pleasure: as in Watteau's *Le Bal*, the dancing figures are a pivot for the charmed world that is so beguilingly presented. The theatre – both the Italian comedy and the legitimate drama – was a fruitful source of inspiration for Watteau and his spiritual heirs, and in the dream-like world of the *fête galante* there seems no clear dividing line between 'amateur' and 'professional' performers.

17 Jean Raoux, *Mademoiselle Prévost as a Bacchante*

18 De Vinck (attrib.), *Court Ballet at Schonbrunn*

17 Jean Raoux, *Mademoiselle Prévost as a Bacchante*. Françoise Prévost made her début at the Paris Opéra in 1699 and was soon recognised as the greatest dancer of her time, succeeding Mademoiselle Subligny (plate 10). This portrait by Raoux is not a literal representation of Prévost as a performer. It subscribes to the mythological conventions which had earned Raoux some of his public favour as a portraitist. The dance attitudes suggested in Prévost's pose and that of the group of bacchantes and satyrs are conventionally antique ones. More than anything else the picture celebrates the delicious femininity of its subject and a discreetly stated sexual charm. Something of the moral standing of the female performer is implied in the identification of Prévost as a bacchante.

18 De Vinck (attrib.), *Court Ballet given at Schonbrunn on January 23, 1765*. In celebration of the marriage of the Emperor Joseph II to Marie Josephine Antoinette of Bavaria in 1765, an allegorical ballet was given by the young members of the royal household. The three central figures are identified as the Archduke Ferdinand, the Archduke Maximilien and the Archduchess Marie Antoinette, while the attendant children are members of the Clary and Auersberg families. The painting is an unusual record of a court 'ballet' after the middle of the eighteenth century. In this case it probably amounted to no more than polite amateur theatricals, in which the royal children and their friends could demonstrate their skill in dancing. The line dividing theatrical dance from social dance was still imprecise.

19 Carle van Loo, *Portrait of Marie Sallé*. Marie Sallé was the contemporary of La Camargo and her exact opposite as an artist. This polarity was best expressed by Voltaire in his famous verses:

Ah, Camargo, que vous êtes brillante,
Mais que Sallé, grands dieux, est ravissante,
Que vos pas sont légers, et que les siens sont doux.
Elle est inimitable et vous toujours nouvelle.
Les nymphes sautent comme vous
Et les graces dansent comme elle.

Sallé, a dramatic dancer, was one of the first to seek some greater truth in stage dress than was habitual at this time: when she staged her own *Pygmalion* in London in 1732 her hair fell naturally on her shoulders and 'Grecian' draperies replaced the traditionally opulent outer garment. Like Camargo she sought reform of dress, but for reasons of artistic conscience rather than vanity. This portrait, variously attributed to Carle van Loo and to his nephew Louis Michel van Loo, reveals the serene charm of a clearly intelligent woman – qualities which impressed her contemporaries.

19 Carle van Loo, *Portrait of Marie Sallé*

20 J. F. Schall, *Marie-Madeleine Guimard*

and rival Marie Sallé made a more radical change in stage dress. Appearing in her own ballet, *Pygmalion*, in London in 1734 she softened formal costume with lighter draperies and dressed her hair in accordance with the antique style in order to suggest some greater realism of character than was usual at this time. This quest for truth was to be a recurring theme of eighteenth-century dance. The attitudes of the opera-ballet had become so rigid that any sort of expressive truth was impossible. Innovators like Sallé, like the Englishman John Weaver, the Austrian Franz Hilferding, his pupil the Italian Gasparo Angiolini and, supremely, the French Jean-Georges Noverre were to strive for the establishment of a freer and more dramatically expressive form by which narrative might be explored in dance. This is the *ballet d'action*, whose theories were to mark the emergence of the choreographer as an important figure in ballet.

The breaking away from the rigid formulae of the opera-ballet can be seen as a reflection of the larger intellectual movement of the Enlightenment in the latter part of the eighteenth century and of the softening of late Baroque grandeur into the charm and delicacy of Rococo. But court attitudes still dominated dance. The male dancer of noble roles was trapped in the ludicrous *tonnelet*, a panniered skirt which might stretch the width of his arms and which had been adapted from the undergarments of medieval knights-at-arms. The female dancer was imprisoned in the ever-widening skirts which reflected the fashion of court dress of the time. The artists' view of dancers was still that of agreeable and highly decorative figures caught in the fantasy landscapes of Watteau, Lancret and Fragonard.

Albeit dance was now officially liberated from the court, its links with court spectacle still remained. The performance in 1745 of *La Princesse de Navarre*, a *comédie-ballet* staged to celebrate the marriage of Louis XV's son to an Infanta of Spain, and immortalised in Cochin's engraving, indicates how magnificent was the theatrical setting for court festivities and how intimate still was the link between the world of the monarchy and its reflection in stage spectacle.

No less flattering to the aspirations of the monarchy were the late Baroque decorations produced by the Bibiena family who, for more than a hundred years, propagated a grandiose style of stage architecture throughout Europe. The soaring, colonnaded complexities that can be seen in the designs by Giuseppe Galli Bibiena presented a magnificent view of palaces which reflected the monarchic ideal of the Habsburgs, whose entertainments he decorated. The collected architectural and perspective designs which Giuseppe Galli dedicated in 1740 to Charles VI, the Holy Roman Emperor, tell a great deal about the princely illusions fostered by the Bibienas. Beautiful, ingenious, they are like superb cages in which the ideas of monarchy were kept.

By the end of the century the theories of Noverre and his colleagues had spread throughout Europe. But at this time the emergence of Neoclassicism as an artistic movement must have seemed inimical to the quest for dramatic truth that lay at the heart of the *ballet d'action*. The ordered calm of Neoclassicism and its reflection of the ideals of the Napoleonic Empire are best seen in the monumental stagings which were given at the Teatro alla Scala in Milan during the early years of the nineteenth century.

The choreographies of Salvatore Viganò, vast heroic mime spectacles, and the designs of Alessandro Sanquirico which so aptly framed them, were based on huge themes like those of *The Titans*, *Joan of Arc* and *Othello*. The true forerunners of Romanticism, however, were Jean Dauberval, the first choreographer of the comic ballet *La Fille mal gardée*, and Charles-Louis Didelot. Didelot's career, spent chiefly in Russia, is a first indication of the quest for aerial flight as an attribute of dancing: in his *Flore et Zéphire*, in which dancers were made to fly on wires, one of the key images of Romanticism is seen for the first time.

The portrayal of dancing by artists at the beginning of the nineteenth century reveals how vast had been the change in costume with the emergence of Neoclassicism and the fashions in dress of Napoleon's Empire. Gone are the huge skirts for women and the decorative exuberance of male costume; instead, an elegant simplicity informs both male and female dress for the stage. Schadow's drawings of Viganò and his wife Maria Medina, Gillray's and Cruickshank's cartoons of Didelot's ballets in London, show how gauzy the ballerina's costumes had now become. The element of lubricity that we sometimes find in Rowlandson is amply evident in the pretty breasts that peep through the dancers' draperies, and the delight in such improbable incidents as members of the bench of bishops inspecting dancers' clothes in the interests of propriety. This alleged immodesty of female dancers' dress caused Captain Gronow, the English diarist, to note on a visit to Milan in 1821 that the dancers at La Scala 'were obliged to wear by order of the [Austrian] police, skyblue pantaloons which reached down to their knees, but were so tight that the outline of the figure was more apparent, and the effect produced more indelicate, than if the usual gauze inexpressibles had been used. What bullies and savages these Austrians are – they even make the dancing girls put on the breeches of their Hungarian infantry.'

21 L. Legoux, *Complimentary ticket for a benefit by Rose Didelot*. 1796. The choreographer Charles-Louis Didelot was one of the most influential figures in the first decades of the nineteenth century. His ballets provided an essential bridge between the eighteenth-century dance and the invasion of the air by the Romantic ballet. Though the crucial years of his career were spent in Russia, he made a series of appearances in London accompanied by his first wife, the radiantly pretty Mademoiselle Rose. For her first benefit performance in London in 1796 a special ticket was engraved. It shows Rose Didelot in the new style of Neoclassic costuming which allowed greater freedom of movement for the female dancer.

22 Gabriel de St Aubin, *Le Bal Paré* (detail)

23 Nicolas Lancret, *Mademoiselle Camargo*

23 Nicolas Lancret, *Mademoiselle Camargo*. Marie-Anne de Cupis de Camargo was born in Brussels and made her début in 1726 at the Paris Opéra where she had been a pupil of Mademoiselle Prévost. A woman of great beauty, charm, vivacity, she was celebrated for the lightness and brilliance of her style as a dancer. Her technical excellence was so considerable that her one time teacher was forced to retire when faced with such competition, and Camargo reigned very prettily in the hearts of her audience. A pride in her technical ability brought about the reform for which she is best remembered: the shortening of floor length skirts to a discreet mid-calf so that her skill in footwork could be seen. Lancret's portrait places her in a Watteauesque setting and offers a convincing record of the dance style of the period and of the costuming.

24 Antoine Pesne, *Portrait of Barbara Campanini*. La Barberina, as she was known, was an Italian dancer of brilliant technique and no less brilliant liaisons. Her lovers ranged from Frederick the Great, for whom she danced in Berlin, to Lord Stuart

24 Antoine Pesne, *Portrait of Barbara Campanini*

25 Thomas Gainsborough, *Giovanna Baccelli*

Mackenzie, with whom she eloped to Venice. It was while she was in Berlin that her undoubted beauty was captured by Pesne, at that time chief painter to Frederick the Great and director of the Berlin Academy. He presents her against a garden setting in the elaborate and ravishing costume of a bacchante, an identification due more to the leopardskin overskirt than to anything else.

25 Thomas Gainsborough, *Giovanna Baccelli*. Giovanna Zanerini, who was born in Venice and made her London début in 1774, was known under her stage name as La Baccelli. Acknowledged as a brilliant dancer as well as a creature of great charm and allure, she is remembered today chiefly through this magnificent portrait by Gainsborough, and through the enchanting marble by Locatelli which shows her reclining nude on a couch. This statue is found at Knole and her connection with that great house comes from her lengthy association with the Duke of Dorset. When the Duke was posted to Paris as British Ambassador, La Baccelli accompanied him and she celebrated his acquisition of the Order of the

Garter in 1788 by appearing on stage with its ribbon as a bandeau round her head. Gainsborough's portrait offers little testimony to her dance ability beyond the delicacy of her pose, but it says everything about her style and the elegance of her appearance for which she was justly celebrated.

26 Louis René Boquet, Costume design

27 P. Lior (attrib.), Costume design

BALLET INTO THE THEATRE

28 Bernardo Bellotto, *Le Turc généreux*

26 Louis René Boquet, Costume design. c. 1750.
The exaggerated span of this skirt suggests how
formalised had become the dress of the female
performer by the mid-eighteenth century. We can
assume that Boquet made this design for some royal
figure in an opera-ballet of the period and it indicates
the fantastication of which Rococo design was
capable. The vast panniered skirts of the female
performer were matched by the *tonnelet* of the male
dancer – small wonder that Noverre was to inveigh
against the improbability of dancers' apparel when
he sought some kind of dramatic reality in ballet.
Boquet's design is typical of the unthinking
development of stage costume to a point where it
leaves any sort of truth behind.

27 P. Lior (attrib.), Design for a male dancer.
c. 1750. Lior, who provided designs for the
opéra-ballets of the mid-eighteenth century, has
here pinpointed much of the improbability in the
appearance of the male performer. The *tonnelet*, a
wired skirt which harked back to the undergarments of knights at arms, was built out on a
frame and at its most extreme could extend to arm's

width. Its effect in performance, as Noverre pointed
out, was to bounce up and down and to distort the
movement of the body. This seemed to matter little
to an audience who accepted this codified appearance of singers and dancers. The adaptation of
Roman armour atop the *tonnelet* only increases the
unlikeliness of this attire.

28 Bernardo Bellotto, *Le Turc généreux*. Engraving.
Bernardo Bellotto, nephew and pupil of Canaletto,
lived in Italy and Prussia before going to Poland,
where he settled in Warsaw and worked for the
King until his death. *Le Turc généreux* was a scene
from *Les Indes galantes*, one of the grandest of Jean-
Phillipe Rameau's opera-ballets. It was first given in
Paris in 1735 and was revived in Vienna in 1758 with
choreography by Franz Hilferding. Staged in
honour of the Turkish envoys' visit to that city, it
remained in the repertory at the Theater am
Kartnertor and so impressed Bellotto when he saw it
on his arrival in Vienna in 1759 that he made a rapid
sketch of its central action in his notebook. This was
incorporated in his finished engraving, a highly
skilled representation of theatrical dance.

29 Gian Domenico Tiepolo, *The Minuet*

30 Carolina Lose after Alessandro Sanquirico, *Interior of a Greenhouse*

31 Jean-Louis Desprez, Setting for *Christine*

29 Gian Domenico Tiepolo, *The Minuet*. Oil. Son of the more celebrated Giovanni Battista, G. D. Tiepolo responded with great affection to the popular theatre and popular entertainments of his time in Venice. In the lovely *Minuet*, now in the Louvre, he presents a whirlpool of activity – of maskers, musicians and observers – round the ravishing central figure of the beautiful girl who gazes so serenely out from the background of grotesques. The sense of movement and the excitement of the scene are most stylishly caught. Tiepolo *fils* is here inspired by one of his father's paintings, dated 1756, now in the Catalonian Museum in Barcelona, in which a very similar Venetian carnival scene is depicted.

30 Carolina Lose after Alessandro Sanquirico, *Interior of a Greenhouse*. Etching and aquatint, 1827. Greatest master of stage design of the Neoclassic period was Alessandro Sanquirico, whose decorations for the operas and ballets staged at the Teatro alla Scala, Milan, in the first decades of the nineteenth century offer brave evidence of the theatre of the time. Completely in harmony with the grandiose aspirations of Neoclassicism, Sanquirico produced decors that can still amaze and delight the eye. This scene from Luigi Henry's ballet *Elerz and Zulmida* of 1826 shows a mime scene set in a gigantic conservatory. The figures of the performers are dwarfed not only by the architectural splendour of the building but also by the exuberance of the plants on the right hand side, which effectively balance the composition of the picture.

31 Jean-Louis Desprez, Setting for *Christine*. The French artist Jean-Louis Desprez went to Stockholm as designer for the court theatre under Gustave III and his watercolour of *Christine*, a comedy with songs and dance, shows the production as it was seen at the Gripsholm Palace Theatre in 1784. Far more than a simple design drawing, the watercolour is valuable testimony to the qualities of court entertainment at the end of the eighteenth century.

32 Gabriel de St Aubin, *Momus*

33 F. Basan after Gabriel de St Aubin, *La Guinguette*

32 Gabriel de St Aubin, *Momus*. Chalk drawing. De St Aubin here presents us with one of the most credible representations of a dancer in the full splendour of feathers and *tonnelet,* which were characteristic of the male dancer's garb in the middle of the eighteenth century. Momus serves to introduce, as his scroll announces, a collection of drawings of the fancy dress worn at a ball at Saint Cloud in 1752.

33 F. Basan after Gabriel de St Aubin, *La Guinguette*. Engraving. De St Aubin was one of the most compelling and lively analysts of Parisian life. The engraving of *La Guinguette* by Basan preserves a scene from a burlesque work with choreography by Jean François de Hesse, which was performed at the Théâtre Italien, in 1750. The Guinguette, a tavern scene, had long been the subject for dance – John Weaver's *Tavern Bilkers* of 1708 is an early forerunner. De Hesse plainly made this scene more polite than earlier, ruder versions, and de St Aubin has also polished the appearance of the performers so that they seem relations of court play-actors who impersonated shepherds and shepherdesses.

34 Giuseppe Galli Bibiena,
Theatrical setting. The Bibiena
family were a dynasty of designers
whose four generations influenced
the appearance of the stage for a
hundred years from the end of the
seventeenth century. The grandeur
and tremendous power of high
Baroque decoration can be
particularly appreciated in the work
of Giuseppe, whose designs for
theatrical performances, for
monuments, and for every kind of
court display, seem to capture the
very spirit of the House of
Habsburg. His setting for the
entertainment staged on the
occasion of the marriage of the
Prince of Poland, Prince Elector of
Saxony, reflects exactly the
grandiose aspirations of his royal
masters. The setting became a
mirror in which the palace itself
acquired a heightened reality.
Against colonnades of false
perspective, the royal audience
could watch their own magnificence
being honoured. Bibiena created a
world of illusion which in turn
fostered the illusions of his princely
employers. This design comes from
a book of architectural and
perspective designs dedicated in
1740 to Charles VI, the Holy
Roman Emperor.

34 Guiseppe Galli Bibiena, Theatrical setting

34

35 After Carmontelle (Louis Carrogis), *Pas de deux from 'Sylvie'*

35 After Carmontelle (Louis Carrogis), *Pas de deux from 'Sylvie'*. Engraving. Carmontelle was both an author and a painter. His enthusiasm for the world in which he lived and his ability to move from the court to the fairground resulted, as Marian Hannah Winter notes in her invaluable *Pre-Romantic Ballet* (London, 1974), in 'a series of gouaches and watercolour sketches which are a unique record of the *ancien régime*'. This engraving of a watercolour sketch shows Jean Dauberval and Marie Allard in the pantomimic duet of the Scythians from the opera-ballet *Sylvie* first produced at the Paris Opéra in 1766, with choreography by Dauberval. Carmontelle records a scene in which the two characters were reportedly declaring their mutual affection. The stylisation of gesture as well as the improbability of costuming reveal how formal and stultified the conventions of theatrical performance had become. Plumes and trailing ivy leaves, leopard skins and elaborate hair styles, still reflect the complexity of performing dress. Each age perpetuates certain conventions about historical appearance. These supposedly antique figures are no more improbable, in fact, than some nineteenth-century versions of the classical world or, indeed, those of our own time in ballet or in the cinema.

36 Charles Nicolas Cochin, *La Princesse de Navarre*. Engraving. The marriage in February 1745 of the Dauphin, son of Louis XV, to the Infanta Marie Thérèse of Spain occasioned a magnificent spectacle. This was *La Princesse de Navarre*, a combination of drama, opera and dance, with a text by Voltaire and music by Rameau. The work was staged in the Riding School of the Grandes Écuries at Versailles and Cochin's engraving is a brilliant record of the final moments of the performance. Splendour is all: the worlds of court and theatre hardly seem separated by the proscenium arch, and the stage spectacle is like a looking glass in which the court may see a flattering reflection of itself.

36 Charles Nicolas Cochin, *La Princesse de Navarre*

37 Francesco Bartolozzi after Nathaniel Dance, *Jason and Medea*

38 Francesco Bartolozzi and Benedetto Pastorini after Nathaniel Dance, *Auguste Vestris*

37 Francesco Bartolozzi after Nathaniel Dance, *Jason and Medea*. Etching and aquatint. The presence in London of Gaetano Vestris and Auguste Vestris, his son by Marie Allard, during the season of 1781 was sufficiently important to produce a considerable series of satirical drawings of them. Their dominant position in European dance could not be more clearly illustrated: both were insufferably vain, but their vanity was excused by their supremacy as performers. In the winter of 1780 father and son appeared at the King's Theatre in the Haymarket. Horace Walpole noted: '. . . It is the universal voice that he (Vestris *père*) is the only perfect being that has dropped from the clouds within the memory of man or woman.' The presence of these two extraordinary dancers (and the public's delight in satiric records of events) occasioned a sequence of broadsheets that testify to their extreme popular impact. Gilray, Sandby and Dance all produced drawings which poke fun at the pair. The illustration opposite is a slightly mocking view of Gaetano as he appeared in Noverre's *Jason and Medea* in June 1781.

38 Francesco Bartolozzi and Benedetto Pastorini after Nathaniel Dance, *Auguste Vestris*. Etching and engraving. Unlike his father, who was a *danseur noble*, Auguste Vestris, with his greater virtuosity, was a *danseur de demi-caractère*. Two engravings show Auguste in this pose: the first, a front view, finds him holding only his hat; the second, illustrated here, is a back view in which the dancer also clutches a bag labelled 'English guineas', while his hat is full of bank notes. The engraving is captioned *Oh qui goose-toe*. The reference to the goose comes from Plutarch's apothegm: a stranger at Sparta standing long on one leg, said to a Lacedaemonian, 'I do not believe you can do as much.' 'True', said he, 'but every goose can.'

A rhyme underneath reads:
He danc'd like a Monkey, his pockets well
  cramm'd:
Caper'd off with a Grin; 'Kiss my A . . . &
  be D . . .'

Despite its intentions as caricature, Dance's drawing is a fine evocation of the agility and technical exuberance that made Auguste the darling of his age and was also to make him one of the most influential teachers in the history of ballet. His life spans the last great years of eighteenth-century dance and the Romantic movement. His final appearance on stage was in a minuet with Marie Taglioni in 1834: the ages of Louis XVI and Louis Philippe were united.

39 *Marie-Madeleine Guimard visiting the sick*

39 *Marie-Madeleine Guimard visiting the sick*. Engraving. Marie-Madeleine Guimard was one of the most remarkable dancers of her time. Her professional career brought her early stardom at the age of twenty as a principal dancer at the Paris Opéra, despite a thinness which had earned her the nickname *La Squelette des Graces*. Privately she was notorious for the succession of rich lovers who kept her in the most splendid luxury, which allowed her to play Lady Bountiful. This print is unusual in that it commemorates a totally untheatrical side of a dancer's life: Guimard's acts of charity were many.

40 James Gillray, *Operational Reform*

41 French paper doll

42 Thomas Rowlandson, *The Prospect Before Us*

40 James Gillray, *Operational Reform*. Engraving, 1798. Gillray's cartoon refers to the scandal when the Bench of Bishops were involved in deciding whether the French dancers at the King's Theatre in London were decently clothed.

41 French paper doll. c. 1750. The *Pantin* – a cut-out paper doll – took its name from a village near Paris in which these toys were first made. Originally intended for children, the *pantin* became a plaything for adults and soon achieved a vogue among the aristocracy in Paris, who were amused to cut out these figures printed on heavy paper or card and then transform them into dancing homuncules by means of thread. The fashion for them became so extreme that even François Boucher was called upon to decorate one, and they were sometimes shown dressed in imitation of the clothing of their owners. Eventually they developed into the more celebrated cut-out toys of the *Imagerie d'Épinal*. The doll reproduced is unusual in that it is made in the image of a *danseur noble* of the mid-eighteenth century – probably a *berger galant* – decked in *tonnelet* and feathered head-dress.

42 Thomas Rowlandson, *The Prospect Before Us*. Coloured etching. Thomas Rowlandson is one of the best guides to the social scene at the turn of the

nineteenth century. No aspect of contemporary life escaped his sharp eye and his even sharper pencil. A master draughtsman, he was also a master of observation. In *The Prospect Before Us* he shows Didelot dancing with Madame Théodore in *Amphion and Thalia* at the Pantheon. The satirical point of this print was the fact that two theatres, the Pantheon and the Haymarket, both claimed royal patronage and the coveted title of 'King's' Theatre. The rivalry between their respective managers, Mr Taylor and Mr O'Reilly, excited a good deal of public amusement. (This competition was to provide even more amusement when used by Ninette de Valois as the subject for her comedy ballet, *The Prospect Before Us*, in 1940.) Rowlandson's view of the scene is characteristically lively, and crammed with grotesque detail. In the royal box, just above Mme Théodore's head, George III, the theatre's patron, is using a spyglass, while his consort Queen Charlotte sits at his side.

43, 44 Gottfried Schadow, Salvatore Viganò and his wife Maria Medina

43, 44 Gottfried Schadow, Salvatore Viganò and his wife Maria Medina. Drawings, c. 1793. Salvatore Viganò is acknowledged as one of the great masters of Italian ballet: his staging of massive mimetic spectacles at the Teatro alla Scala, Milan, established a vogue for such entertainments, which were enhanced by the decoration of Sanquirico (plate 30). His early career was spent touring Europe and he first achieved fame as a dancer with his wife, Maria Medina, in their pantomimic duets which they performed in Vienna. In Schadow's drawings we sense a new elegance of costuming and a new freedom of movement. Neoclassicism has brought gauzy draperies and laced sandals for Maria Medina, and an admirable simplicity to Viganò's dress.

45 Johann Heinrich Füssli (Fuseli), *Two dancers*. Pencil and black chalk, c. 1814. Fuseli, who was Swiss-born but made his career in England, is one of the most interesting forerunners of Romanticism. In his paintings many of the night-mare and irrational aspects of Romanticism are to be seen, but he was also an outstanding illustrator of works of literature, being inspired by Shakespeare, Milton, the Bible and Dante. And it is from Dante that he took the idea of the two figures shown in this pencil and black chalk drawing. It is noteworthy for an observer today in the modernity of its pose and in its suggestion of very advanced *pas de deux* work. The position is not one lightly taken even now and the drawing represents an imaginative rather than an actual view of a performance. It is prophetic, and like the many dance poses that can be seen in the drawings of Fuseli's contemporary, William Blake, it shows beautiful movement 'frozen' at its most essential moment.

45 Johann Heinrich Fuseli, *Two dancers*

THE ROMANTIC MOVEMENT

The week I arrived in Petersburg was the last of the season at the Grand Opera; I had the pleasure of enjoying some toe-pointed stanzas of the poetry of motion as rendered by the agile limbs of the renowned Russian dancer, Mlle Bagdanov. The Russians are deliriously proud of this favoured child of Terpsichore . . . Last spring she was more the rage than ever. Her portrait, lithographed, was in all the printsellers' windows.

George Augustus Sala *A Journey due North*

Romanticism came late to ballet. The Romantic movement had its roots in the eighteenth century; in music, literature and painting its fine fervours can be traced to the last years of Napoleon's reign as master of Europe. The writings and compositions of E. T. A. Hoffman, the paintings of Géricault, the *Fantastic Symphony* of Berlioz, the *Meditations* of Lamartine and the piano music of Chopin had all established the ideals of Romanticism long before Marie Taglioni, the presiding divinity of the Romantic ballet, appeared on stage. The battle call of Romanticism in the theatre came with the celebrated first night of Victor Hugo's *Hernani* in 1830. In the following year the ballet scene in Meyerbeer's opera *Robert the Devil* showed the spectral figures of white-clad nuns, led by Taglioni, dancing in the moonlight in a ruined cloister. Here were the ingredients for the Romantic ballet: the female form swathed in gauze; mystery and the supernatural. Adolphe Nourrit, the leading tenor in the opera, had the wit to see that Taglioni seemed the very incarnation of the Romantic female. He suggested to Taglioni's choreographer father an idea for a ballet which took practical form in the following year with the first performance of *La Sylphide* at the Paris Opéra. For the next twenty years, during the heyday of the Romantic dance, the ballerina was to reign supreme. Such divinities as Taglioni, Carlotta Grisi, Fanny Elssler, Fanny Cerrito and Lucile Grahn dominated the stages of Europe, and imposed an image upon dancing which has yet to be totally dispelled. The pictorial records of the ballet of this period give a marvellously precise idea of the impact which the ballerina had upon the public. Gone was the dominance of the male dancer in the eighteenth century. The new, often bourgeois

46 John Brandard, *Lucile Grahn in 'Catarina'*. Lithograph, 1846. *Catarina or The Bandit's Daughter* was one of the several important full-length ballets staged in London by Jules Perrot at Her Majesty's Theatre. It was inspired by an incident in the life of the painter Salvatore Rosa, and its most famous dance was the *Pas Stratégique* in which the heroine, as Ivor Guest vividly describes in his *Romantic Ballet in England* (London, 1954), 'instructs her brigands in musket drill and military evolutions, which ended with the *corps de ballet* climbing up the rocks, then rushing down fiercely towards the audience, pointing their muskets at the unfortunate Monsieur Nadaud, who was conducting the orchestra'. Brandard was one of several artists producing very appealing records of the Romantic ballet.

47 *Marie Taglioni in 'La Sylphide'*

audience sought a theatre of heightened emotion and escapism, and this the Romantic ballet gave them, and this the artists of the period in turn depicted. The etherealisation of the female was reflected in the gradual emergence of *pointe* work – dancing on the very tips of the toes – which was intended to show the Romantic ballerina maintaining minimum contact with the ground. The popularity of ballet is reflected in the massive output of lithographs and prints which celebrate the imponderable charms of these goddesses of the age. Floating through the air, poised weightless upon a flower, caught in a variety of enchanting attitudes as supposed gypsies or Lithuanians or Spanish beauties, as ondines and naiads and wilis, the Romantic dancer is a creature of entrancing grace and prettiness, and complete improbability. Her dress is formalised in its reliance upon a bell-shaped skirt and light slippers upon her ideally narrow feet; the addition of a pair of wings, a saucy hat or a coronet of flowers, a beribboned bodice or pearl bracelets, are token suggestions of national or magical identity. But essentially and inescapably she is the ballerina, the adorable female, doe-eyed and deliciously rounded of forearm. As partner, or set discreetly in the background, the male dancer had been put in his place – a place he did not leave for nearly a hundred years, when Vaslav Nijinsky and Adolf Bolm announced, during the *Saison Russe* of 1909, that the *danseur* had a positive identity in ballet once again.

In an age when most women were trapped in the home as wives and mothers, the 'liberated' figure of the ballerina reflects both her unusual physical freedom and also the fact of her dubious social position. It was a commonplace that dancers were not 'respectable', yet nevertheless their popularity was intense. Their image was to be found in prints, in porcelain; the name of the Sylphide advertised parasols; stage coaches were called after dancers; the ballerinas were fêted wherever they went. Even Queen Victoria doted upon the ballet, and at her behest two of the most celebrated ballerinas were brought together in the delicate rivalry of a *pas de deux*.

From its initial burst of activity in Paris the ideals of the Romantic ballet spread swiftly throughout Europe and to the United States, thanks to the peregrinations of ballerinas and choreographers. In London during the 1840s the presence of Jules Perrot, greatest choreographer of the period, brought a golden age of ballet which was not to return for another hundred years. Taglioni's visits to Russia were generally accredited with having revived a flagging public interest in the ballet, and when Jules Perrot worked at the Bolshoy Theatre in St Petersburg for a decade in the 1850s he initiated the greatest era of the Imperial Ballet. Fanny Elssler excited vast admiration wherever she travelled: in Washington, Congress adjourned its sessions early so that its members might attend her performances. In Moscow her final appearance earned her more than three hundred bouquets and the attentions of the secret police into the verses celebrating her talents.

The prints and lithographs of the Romantic ballet that emerged during the heyday of the 1830s and 1840s represent, inevitably, something of what we may call Victorian taste. Certainly some of the finest examples – the work of Chalon and Brandard – proclaim those virtues of poetical grace and airy delicacy which we can also find in the music of that darling of the early Victorians, Felix Mendelssohn-Bartholdy. With their remarkable technical finesse, their clear, light colours and apposite pinpointing of a pose or a movement, these lithographs are works of art of unquestioned merit. Brandard and Chalon were both adept at catching what we assume to be a very good 'likeness' of the dancer; other artists – Bouvier, for example – tend rather more to generalisation, in an art form which at worst we must reproach with generalising about the identity of the ballerina as a symbol of femininity. But the delicious freedom of some of the poses, the happy way in which movement has often been captured, mark these lithographs as convincing testimony to the gifts of the performers they hymn. At their very finest, in Chalon's series of portraits of Marie Taglioni, we do indeed know something about 'Marie pleine de grace', about her gentleness and sweetness of expression, about her phenomenal lightness and the lovely fragility of her style. Like Baron de Meyer's superb sequence of photographs of Nijinsky taken in London during 1911, we sense the reality of movement, and the force of a temperament uniquely great which still haunts dancers and audiences today.

In Italy, as in France, Romanticism lost its impetus by the mid-century. Curiously, in the backwater of Denmark the presence of a great choreographer and dancer, August Bournonville, ensured a continuity of interest through his considerable output of ballets and the great system of training – inherited from his teacher Auguste Vestris – that he established in the Royal Theatre in Copenhagen.

In Russia the entire development of choreography during the nineteenth century was due to a series of French ballet masters. Didelot had created major works in the early years of the century; Jules Perrot and Arthur Saint-Léon enriched the repertory in subsequent years; in 1869 Marius Petipa became chief ballet master and ruled with absolute power until 1903. Petipa had arrived in Russia as a dancer in 1847; thereafter his career was placed entirely at the service of the Imperial Ballet and it is to him that we must ascribe the supremacy of the Russian Ballet in the last years of the nineteenth century.

The waning of interest in ballet as an art form in much of western Europe, which came with the fading of the Romantic movement, is reflected in the absence of any really significant pictorial material. It was only with the emergence of Impressionism and the desire to depict what the eye actually sees that we find artists, fascinated in recording the complexities of movement, renewing an interest in dance and the dancer. It is ironic that what Degas was to record was ballet in decline.

48 Constantin Guys, *Dans les Coulisses*. Pen and wash. Guys was one of the most perceptive analysts of nineteenth-century life. Baudelaire, in his study, *The Painter of Modern Life*, said of him: 'His interest is the whole world; he wants to know, understand and appreciate everything that happens on the surface of our globe . . . The crowd is his element, as the air is that of birds and water of fishes. His passion and his profession are to become one flesh with the crowd.' Guys captured both the pageantry and squalor of Parisian life during the period of the Second Empire, and inevitably the women of that world – both the whores and the grand ladies in their crinolines – are immortalised in his work.

49 Jules Collignon, *Giselle*

49 Jules Collignon, *The Second Act of 'Giselle'*.
Steel engraving, 1844. *Giselle* is the apogee of
Romanticism. In its second act the midnight forest,
the mysterious Wilis and the floating figure of the
lost beloved epitomise the Romantic ideal. This
engraving, though not literal, conveys exactly the
spirit of the work. *Les Beautés de l'Opéra*, from which
this illustration comes, was a souvenir book
produced in Paris which contained illustrated essays
on nine of the most famous operas and ballets of the
Romantic period. The great popularity of these same
works in London occasioned an English edition
which was dedicated 'with the profoundest respect'
to Queen Victoria. Her Majesty's affection for the
ballet dated from her childhood and in 1843, when
asked what items it would please her to see on a
State visit to the theatre, she requested a *pas de deux*
which would feature two of London's darlings,
Fanny Elssler and Fanny Cerrito. This sparked off
the succession of ballerina displays which took place
later in the decade, when Taglioni, Grisi, Cerrito,
Grahn and Rosati were all variously deployed in
those *divertissements* by Jules Perrot that were
described by the rival choreographer Saint Léon as
'steeple-chases'.

50 Eichens after Paul Bürde, *Marie-Paul Taglioni*

50 Eichens after Paul Bürde, *Marie-Paul Taglioni*. Lithograph. Marie-Paul Taglioni was the daughter of Paul Taglioni and niece of the greater Marie whose name she bears. Her father presented her in London in several ballets, among which *Thea or the Flower Fairy* (1847) was the most successful. Eichens' lithograph of Bürde's painting accepts the Romantic convention of showing the dancer barefoot. Marie-Paul Taglioni's role as the flower fairy is charmingly suggested in her costuming and in the slightly sentimentalised setting among bedewed roses. Yet the innocence of the presentation avoids any suggestion of kitsch. In an unsophisticated age both artist and public were prepared to believe in this identification of a dancer with her role. It is nice to record that Marie-Paul Taglioni married extremely well, becoming the wife of the immensely noble Prince Joseph Windisch-Grätz.

51 Angelo Inganni, Portrait captioned 'La danzatrice Maria Taglioni'. This mysterious portrait of a dancer in her dressing room is improbably identified as Marie Taglioni. In a discussion of the painting in *Dance and Dancers* in May 1963, the late Cyril Beaumont made out a very good case for its being Marie-Paul Taglioni. It is an unexpectedly frank portrayal of a dancer, more an excuse for a study of a beautiful nude than a record of a performer. The dancer, preparing for a performance, has been cast as Venus in what must have seemed an updated version of the Toilet of Venus. The duenna and the attendant dresser all contribute to the erotic quality of the painting.

51 Angelo Inganni, *La danzatrice Maria Taglioni*

52 *The Wags of Wapping*

52 *The Wags of Wapping*. Engraving, 1846. *The Illustrated London News* published this record of the ballet staged at the Theatre Royal, Drury Lane, London in the mid century. The ballerina is Sophia Fucco, who was nicknamed *La Pointue* because of the strength of her *pointe* work.

53 Achille Devéria, *La Gipsy*, Act II. Lithograph. First staged at the Paris Opéra in January 1839, the immensely successful *La Gipsy*, a ballet by Joseph Mazilier, was conceived as a vehicle for Fanny Elssler. Elssler was Marie Taglioni's only real rival, offering the other side of the Romantic coin, dramatic vivacity and a lustrous physical presence: Gautier spoke of Taglioni as a 'Christian' and of Elssler as a 'Pagan' dancer. *La Gipsy* was no more silly in its plot than many another work of the period. It involved gypsies, a stolen baby, the market place in Edinburgh and one of the most intriguing characters in all ballet, Narcisse de Crakentorp – 'Lord Campbell's nephew and a conceited fool'. Devéria's lithograph is of a later cast – Adèle Dumilâtre and Eugène Coralli – and it conveys something of the dramatic vitality and

energy which marked this ballet. It is a compelling record of stage action and without the marmorial daintiness of some Romantic iconography.

54 *Fanny Cerrito in 'Ondine'*. Steel engraving from the *Illustrated London News*, 1843. Baudelaire records that Guys provided drawings which were engraved for the *Illustrated London News*, a journal which regularly depicted the theatrical events of the time. It remains a treasure house for the historian concerned with ballet. The conventions of its ballet drawings during the Romantic period were fantasticated – the ballerinas had feet which were shaped to perfect and delicate points – but nevertheless the atmosphere of the performance was captured. In 1843 Fanny Cerrito, the darling of London, appeared in *Ondine*, a ballet by Jules Perrot. Its *pas de l'ombre*, in which the water sprite danced with her own shadow, was an instant sensation and became a favourite subject for artists of the period.

53 Achille Devéria, *La Gipsy*

54 *Fanny Cerrito in 'Ondine'*

55 Marie-Alexandre Alophe, *Carlotta Grisi and Lucien Petipa in 'La Péri'*

55 Marie-Alexandre Alophe, *Carlotta Grisi and Lucien Petipa in 'La Péri'*. Lithograph. *La Péri* was first staged at the Paris Opéra in 1843 and its most exciting moment was that in which Grisi had to leap from a six foot platform into the arms of Petipa. The public became obsessed with this feat of derring-do and Ivor Guest in his *Romantic Ballet in Paris* (London, 1966) records that on one occasion when the leap failed to come off the audience obliged Grisi to repeat it three times before they would applaud her. In London, on the other hand, the public begged her not to repeat it when it had misfired. Guest also notes that one gentleman was so convinced that the leap would prove fatal that he would not miss a single performance at the Opéra so that he might be present at her death. Alophe's lithograph captures the moment of this leap which became an understandably popular subject for print-makers.

56 J. Arnout, *The Interior of the Paris Opéra*. Lithograph, c. 1860. A series of handsome coloured lithographs of Paris buildings at the time of the Second Empire by the Arnout family are impressive records of the life in that gilded age. This interior of the Paris Opéra shows the ballet of the nuns from the fourth act of Meyerbeer's opera *Robert le Diable* which had remained in the repertory since 1831. It is worth noting that the stalls were exclusively given over to the gentlemen, while the fashionable ladies disposed themselves in the loges.

57 *Fanny Elssler*. Popular print, c. 1850. Fanny Elssler's triumphs throughout her career were as prodigious as those of any Romantic star. The illustration is a German popular print which satirises that ideal tribute to an artist when the horses are unhitched from her coach and she is drawn in triumph through the streets by an army of admirers.

56 J. Arnout, *The Interior of the Paris Opéra*

57 *Fanny Elssler*

58 J. Bouvier, *Adèle Dumilâtre and Henri Desplaces in 'Le Corsaire'*

59 Edward Morton after S. M. Joy, *Lucile Grahn in 'Eoline, ou la Dryade'*

58 J. Bouvier, *Adèle Dumilâtre and Henri Desplaces in 'Le Corsaire'*. Lithograph, 1844. *The Corsair* was adapted from Byron's poem by several choreographers for the ballet stage. Bouvier's lithograph is of especial interest in that it shows two dancers in correct academic positions and it illuminates the partnering of the period – the pose is unusual for its time. Bouvier has caught the dancers with almost photographic precision in a difficult lift. The absence of any kind of effort and a certain naïveté of style suggest yet again the supposedly imponderable nature of the ballerina.

59 Edward Morton after S. M. Joy, *Lucile Grahn in 'Eoline, ou la Dryade'*. Lithograph, 1845. Another of the divinities of the Romantic Ballet was Lucile Grahn. Danish-born, Grahn was a pupil of August Bournonville and it was for her that he staged his version of *La Sylphide* in Copenhagen in 1836. *Eoline* was one of the ballets in which she endeared herself to the London audience – it was staged at Her Majesty's Theatre in 1845 – and it tells of a wood sprite who falls in love with a mortal and dies on her wedding day. The lithograph presents an entirely typical view of a Romantic ballerina: it is not 'true' to Grahn save in its approximation of her features, but it is true to the image which her dancing was supposed to arouse in the public mind and true to

the qualities of the character she interpreted. Lithographs such as these abounded, serving as reminders of a theatrical experience. In her later years Grahn lived in Germany where she choreographed the dance scenes in some of Wagner's operas – and the master approved of her work.

60 John Brandard, Carlotta Grisi in *La Péri*. Lithograph. The Italian-born ballerina, Carlotta Grisi, was the pupil and mistress of Jules Perrot and the favourite dancer of the poet Théophile Gautier. He wrote for her the libretto of *Giselle* in which she created the title role.

60 John Brandard, *Carlotta Grisi in 'La Péri'*

61 Eugène Lami, *Au foyer de l'Opéra*

61 Eugène Lami, *Au foyer de l'Opéra*. 1841. Lami's
view of the green room of the Paris Opéra is an
imaginary gathering which provides a souvenir of
the Romantic movement at its height. Bringing
together some of the dancers and the habitués of the
foyer de la danse, as well as the administrators, it
pinpoints more accurately than strict representation
the atmosphere of what must have seemed in later
years a golden age. Among the personalities
involved are Alfred de Musset, Dr Véron, formerly
director of the Opera, Fanny Elssler and Adèle
Dumilâtre.

62 Marie-Alexandre Alophe, *Carolina Rosati in 'Le
Corsaire'*. Lithograph, c. 1856. With the decline of
the Romantic movement in the middle of the
nineteenth century, ballet performances in Western
Europe stood a poor second to opera. An important
series of lithographs of the ballerinas at the Paris
Opéra appeared in the 1850s, but they were expressly
offered as portrayals of the costumes of the principal
ballets of the time and were sold by the fashion
magazine *Les Modes Parisiennes*. In this opulent
period of the Second Empire, the ballerina was
acquiring public status as an obvious clothes horse.

63 Richard Buckner, *Adeline Plunkett*. Oil, 1844. The
Belgian dancer Adeline Plunkett was a visitor to
London in the 1840s and 1850s where her dancing,
her temperament and her beauty were equally
newsworthy.

62 Marie-Alexandre Alophe, *Carolina Rosati in 'Le
Corsaire'*

63 Richard Buckner, *Adeline Plunkett*

64 Borrell after Charlemagne, *The Naiad and the Fisherman*

65 Paul Gavarni, *In The Wings*

66 Regnier after Belin, *L'Opéra*

64 Borrell after Charlemagne, *The Naiad and the Fisherman*. Lithograph. This Russian lithograph provides a charming record of an incident of royal patronage. On June 16, 1851, the artists of the Imperial Ballet were commissioned to appear in the gardens of the Peterhof outside St Petersburg. A small stage had been built over the surface of the lake in the palace's grounds and Jules Perrot, then a ballet master in St Petersburg, revived part of his *Ondine* for this open air performance in honour of the birthday of the Grand Duchess Olga. Carlotta Grisi, who had been discovered in Naples as a young dancer by Perrot and whose career had been launched by him, was a guest artist with the Imperial Ballet and she appeared in the role of the Ondine, with Perrot himself as the fisherman who loves her. The natural charm of the setting gave a very special attraction to the performance, and the *corps de ballet* of naiads were brought across the lake in little boats shaped like shells.

65 Paul Gavarni, *In the Wings*. Lithograph. Gavarni's record of the world of the Second Empire is frank and unembarrassed in presenting the moral climate of its time. His revellers at public balls, his artists and models and grisettes, are the stuff of *La Vie de*

Bohème. The interview that he captures in the wings of a popular theatre is entirely unromantic. The ballet girl's gauzy skirt reveals everything of her limbs, and we may assume that the gentleman's interest is not only in her dancing. 'Twas ever thus.

66 Regnier after Belin, *L'Opéra*. Lithograph, c. 1850. This is one of a pair of lithographs produced in the 1850s and published both in Paris and New York, which offer scenes from an unidentified Spanish ballet. The purpose of the lithograph is to capitalise on a good deal of Spanish posing by very attractive girls. The deliciously rounded arms and bosoms and calves, the prettiness of the costuming, are far more the subject of the artist's attention than the dance itself. Ballet is now being offered to a wider public as a sanctification of voyeurism.

67 Alfred Edward Chalon, *At the Opera*

68 Bettanier frères after Teichel, *A Roomful of Rats*

67 Alfred Edward Chalon, *At the Opera*. Engraving, 1839. A less enchanted view of the Romantic goddesses than that presented in the lithographs of the period comes from a literary curiosity of the time. The relationship between Lady Blessington and the dandyish Count d'Orsay was somewhat frayed by d'Orsay's predilection for actresses and ballerinas. Lady Blessington took some slight revenge in her lengthy ode *The Belle of the Season*:

> *Brisk music gayer scenes announces,*
> *And in a half dressed danseuse bounces,*
> *With arms that wreathe, and eyes that swim,*
> *And drapery that scarce shades each limb . . .*
> *When Mary saw her vault in air,*
> *Her snow white tunic leaving bare*
> *Her limbs – and heard the deafening shout*
> *Grow louder as she twirled about,*
> *With one leg pointing towards the sky*
> *As if the gallery to defy:*
> *Surprised, and shocked, she turned away,*
> *Wondering how woman e'er could stay,*
> *And thinking men must sure be frantic*
> *Who patronised such postures antic:*

> *She felt abashed to meet the eye*
> *Of every fop that loitered by:*
> *And, oh! how rudely did it vex*
> *Her fresh, pure heart, to mark her sex*
> *Thus outraged, while the noblest came*
> *To gaze and revel in their shame . . .*

Chalon provided a not inapposite contrast between the Victorian young lady sniffing her bouquet and the figure of Fanny Cerrito who is seen in a characteristic pose.

68 Bettanier frères after Teichel, *A Roomful of Rats*. Lithograph, c. 1860. The Paris Opéra was notoriously a happy hunting ground for men of all ages in search of female companionship. The liaisons that resulted were to provide material for novels, plays and a cascade of lithographs which pinpointed exactly contemporary morality. For the girls, the opportunity of a rich lover was sometimes the main reason for their entering the dancing profession. The 'rats' of Teichel's title were the *corps de ballet* girls, and the double demands of a ballet master and of an admirer are cleverly indicated.

69 Gustave Doré, *The Lions' Pit*

69 Gustave Doré, *The Lions' Pit*. Lithograph.
Balletomania had two distinct forms in the
nineteenth century. In Russia, where the word
originated in the 1800s, it implied an obsession with
ballet and with certain dancers whose careers were
followed with intense and all consuming enthusiasm.
In St Petersburg balletomanes acquired a pair of
Taglioni's shoes, had them cooked with a special
sauce and consumed them as best they could. In
Paris, the word suggested rather the Jockey Club's
attitude to dance: a show by pretty girls who were
variously mistresses and mothers but never wives. It
was the Jockey Club who disrupted the first Paris
performance of *Tannhäuser* with determined shouts
for 'le bal-let: le bal-let', because they had arrived
too late at the theatre to witness the dancing that had
been interpolated early in the opera for their benefit.
Doré captures the fanatical enthusiasm and the
sexual interest of the *abonnés* (the season ticket
holders) in the dancing girls.

70 Gustave Doré, *Les Rats de l'Opéra*. Lithograph.
Doré's caricature speaks for itself: a line of pretty
girls fully aware of the gentlemen in the box and the

gentlemen no less aware of the girls. It is an entirely
realistic view of the relationship between dancers
and audience in the middle of the nineteenth
century. Gavarni, Daumier and de Beaumont, as
well as Doré, all produced lithographs which
explored this relationship.

71 William Makepeace Thackeray, *Flora Bemoans the
Absence of Zephyr*, 1836. Unexpectedly, Thackeray
was a balletomane and he gave practical evidence of
this enthusiasm in a small book of caricatures
entitled *Flore et Zephyr* which was published in
London in 1836, supposedly drawn by 'Theophile
Wagstaff'. Like *The Yellowplush Papers* and *The Rose
and the Ring*, it shows Thackeray's delight in satiric
fantasy. Ivor Guest has identified the performances
which inspired Thackeray as those which featured
Taglioni in London in the early 1830s. In a letter
Thackeray noted that Taglioni had 'the most superb
pair of pins', and his drawing of her bewailing
Zephyr's absence conveys very accurately something
of the ritual aspect of dancing, whereby an extension
of the leg into second position is supposed to
express an emotion.

70 Gustave Doré, *Les Rats de l'Opéra*

71 Thackeray, *Flora Bemoans the Absence of Zephyr*

72 George Cruickshank, *Maria Mercandotti*

73 Lorenz, *Giselle*

72 George Cruikshank, *Maria Mercandotti*. Satiric print, 1823. The Earl of Fife was a great admirer of ballet and of ballet dancers. During his service in the Peninsular War he made the acquaintance of a Spanish lady and in 1819 he brought her daughter, the fifteen-year old dancer, Maria Mercandotti, to England. His relationship with her is not clear, but he certainly acted as her patron, and her subsequent success owed much to Lord Fife's protection and interest. Mercandotti's beauty attracted a good many suitors, some encouraged by the fact that Lord Fife had announced that he would settle £15,000 on her when she made a suitable marriage. A leading contender was Mr Hughes Ball who initially offered her an annual income of £2,000. Successive rejections of his offers increased his bids and eventually drove him to tendering both his hand and his entire fortune, which amounted to the then astronomical sum of £25,000 a year (hence his nickname 'Golden Balls'). Mercandotti accepted. The whole intrigue was, of course, public knowledge and occasioned a series of gleeful prints which delighted in Lord Fife's canniness, Hughes' ardour (there is a nice *double entendre* in 'Golden Balls'' supposed comment) and Mercandotti's astuteness.

73 Lorenz, *Giselle* parody. 1841. The excesses of the ballet were meat and drink to the satiric papers in Paris, and in one of them – *The Musée Philipon* – a

74 Alfred Edward Chalon, *Mademoiselle Athalie and Josephine Hullin in 'Le Carnaval de Venise'*

whole section was devoted to *Giselle* when the ballet was first staged. The illustration, which affords a welcome counterbalance to the idealisation of dancers in lithographs, shows a view of the *pas de deux* in Act I between Giselle and Loys. The accompanying text reads '*Oh, la la!* It's stylish dancing, expressive dancing . . . sobbing kneecaps, impassioned calves, weeping arms. It's cramped feet, elegaic ronds de jambes; it's fudge! – fudge, the delight of young ladies in boarding schools, but calm fudge, grand, noble and imposing!'

74 Alfred Edward Chalon, *Mademoiselle Athalie and Josephine Hullin in 'Le Carnaval de Venise'*. Drawing, 1830. Besides providing a beautiful record of the divinities of the Romantic period, Alfred Chalon reveals another side of his character in a series of lampoons which he made in the years immediately before Taglioni altered the course of dancing. Without being savage, and sustained by a very nice understanding of dance technique, Chalon pinpoints

some of the posturings and affectations of the dancers and singers of the time. The caricature of Athalie and Hullin is arguably more accurate – because less idealised – than the polished and proper records that were later to be made of the Romantic dance.

Marie Taglioni. Pages 66–67

Marie Taglioni was the incarnation of Romanticism in dance. Her style, her physical appearance, her qualities as an artist, were to be responsible for a most profound change in the art of dancing. The thin and delicately boned daughter born to Filippo Taglioni, an Italian ballet master, must have seemed improbable material from which a great dancer was to be made. Yet rigorous training and an extremely acute understanding of what she could do best, as well as a flawless technique, eventually made Taglioni the supreme dancer of her time, and one whose image is still today central to the dancing of every ballerina. Taglioni's lightness, her ease, her grace of manner and demure charm, seemed the most beautiful realisation of the Romantic dream of spiritualised femininity. When in 1832 she appeared as La Sylphide she established an image for ballet dancing which it has not yet cast off.

To the new middle class audience of the 1830s Taglioni's qualities were exactly right as an example of womanhood: grace, delicacy, respectability were the chaste aspects of her style. That she floated and barely touched the ground suggests how unreal was man's vision of an unattainable beloved. Every representation we have of her argues a delicious modesty – she was the Victorian Miss etherealised. Her dancing was unquestionably sustained by the most brilliant and carefully studied technique of her time – she would labour half an hour in class repeating a single step – but its effects were not for bravura, but for ease, lightness and that quality, which first beguiled her viewers, of 'a young girl dancing in the ballroom of her father's house'. This intriguing combination of theatrical magic and eminently respectable presence (a marked contrast to the boisterous charms of the ladies who preceded and followed her) caught the public's imagination throughout Europe, and held it. Her career, spanning twenty-five years, found her supremacy as a dancer unchallenged. After her retirement, she was seen as a highly respectable figure (her brief marriage to the unappealing Count Gilbert des Voisins produced one daughter) but her later years were haunted by poverty. A few years before her death she was reduced to teaching the politer ballroom dances to well born English girls.

75 François G. G. Le Paulle, *Marie Taglioni and her brother James in 'La Sylphide'*. Oil, 1834

76 Achille Devéria and Henri Grevedon after August Barre, *Marie Taglioni as La Sylphide*. Lithograph, c. 1837

77 Templeton after Alfred Edward Chalon, *Marie Taglioni as La Sylphide*. Lithograph, 1845

78 *Taglioni*. Stained glass window, c. 1850

79 August Barre, *Marie Taglioni as La Sylphide*. Bronze, 1837

80 *Lola Montez sails for America.* Popular print. Lola Montez was an Irish adventuress and self-styled Spanish dancer who had a vastly successful career as a courtesan. The highpoint of her life was her liaison with King Ludwig I of Bavaria. Thereafter she travelled the world lecturing on the care of the bust, horsewhipping an Australian editor and finally devoting herself to care of fallen women. This cartoon contains some very astute comments upon Lola's character. In the swan boat, with Cupid at the stern aiming his arrows at moping European royalties, Lola blows farewell kisses to the Old World. Her life style in the New World was described by Dr Thomas Nichols, who met her in New York in 1852, as bizarre. 'In the first floor drawing room I found a monkey, three dogs, a parrot, a mocking bird, a Polish prince, a Hungarian count, a bundle of cigarettes, a box of cigars, a decanter of brandy, and Lola Montez, Countess of Landsfeldt . . . who, between puffs of her cigarette, conversed with her visitors in three or four languages, caressed her dogs, scolded her monkey, and was as lively, sparkling, amiable, and rattle-headed as she knew how to be.'

81 Eugenio Latilla, *Three Siamese Grotesques.* 1825. The tradition of grotesque dancing dates back to the very origins of ballet, when acrobatics were introduced as a contrast to nobler forms of dance. This nineteenth-century print by a dancer-turned-artist is of three grotesques in 'The Funeral Dance of Siamese Jugglers' which could have featured in pantomimes well into the present century.

82 *The Black Crook.* Poster, c. 1866. *The Black Crook* must go down in history as the longest running musical entertainment of all time, having notched up forty years of performances in New York. Based upon a nonsensical melodrama, it was developed into an extravaganza of song and dance which opened in Niblo's Gardens in New York in 1866. Its appeal to the public was that irresistible combination of spectacle and naughtiness. Considerable sums were spent on scenery and a 'great Parisienne ballet troupe' was much touted. Rumours that something like nudity would be on view attracted an eager male audience and any female members of the public were reported to be wearing heavy veils to conceal their faces. The poster indicates how costuming for the chorus was as explicit as possible in revealing the nether limbs. Plainly it was the element of 'boldness' that ensured public interest. That some of the dancing might have merit was almost incidental.

80 *Lola Montez sails for America*

81 Eugenio Latilla, *Three Siamese Grotesques*

82 *The Black Crook*

83 Alfred Edward Chalon (attrib.), *The Three Graces*

84 *Behind the Curtain*

83 Alfred Edward Chalon (attrib.), *The Three Graces*. Lithograph, c. 1840. This charming group is not from any one ballet. It is a fantasy representing the three chief graces of the Romantic era as London best loved them. On the left Taglioni is seen as the Sylphide; in the centre is Fanny Elssler dressed in her Cachucha costume from *Le Diable boîteux*; and on the right Carlotta Grisi is seen in the *Pas de Diane* from *La Jolie Fille de Gand*. The lithograph is something of a curiosity. The imaginary linking of these three dancers is not surprising – during the 1840s concatenations of stars were brought on to the stage of Her Majesty's Theatre to vast public enthusiasm – but the costuming of both Taglioni and Grisi has been much amended. Taglioni's dress is shorter; Grisi's is abbreviated to a point of immodesty to Victorian eyes and her bared breast is unthinkable on the stage at that time. The bare feet of these two dancers represent a convention rather than actuality. The public eye was prepared to accept this fantastication of the female performer. No lithographs of the Romantic era pretend to truth of representation. The exquisitely tapered feet, the delicate balance, the notions of flight and the prettily rounded but unmuscular limbs foster illusions about dancing and about womanhood. The Romantic ballerina was never truthfully represented save in the occasional portrait of her as a woman rather than a dancing character.

84 *Behind the Curtain*. Popular print, c. 1880. There was no continuity of ballet tradition in London, and after the high summer of Romanticism stage dancing swiftly fell into bad habits as part of the entertainment in pantomime and music halls. Albert Smith's *Natural History of the Ballet Girl* (London, 1847) is a curious and very revealing document which gives intriguing insights into the drudgery and pathos of dancers' lives, those 'pretty trim-built girls, with sallow faces and large eyes – the pallor that overspreads their features resulting from cosmetics and late hours'.

85 C. Mittag after Paul Bürde, *Fanny Cerrito in 'La Esmeralda'*. Lithograph, 1847. *La Esmeralda* was one of the greatest of Jules Perrot's ballets, inspired by Victor Hugo's novel *Notre Dame de Paris*. Bürde's deliciously improbable painting shows Fanny Cerrito with various appurtenances of the drama: Esmeralda's pet goat; the letters with which she has spelled out the name of her beloved, Phoebus; a distant prospect of Notre Dame itself through the archway and a small dagger tucked into the waistband of her dress. It is an appealing evocation of a radiantly pretty woman who was a darling of the Romantic Age and who did not die until the spring of 1909 – at the moment when Diaghilev brought the Russian Ballet to Paris.

85 C. Mittag after Paul Bürde, *Fanny Cerrito in 'La Esmeralda'*

THE WORLD
OF DEGAS

In the evening the Muses do not discuss, they dance.
Paul Valéry quoting Edgar Degas

The Impressionist movement in the 1860s sought to capture what the eye sees. Of one of its founders Cézanne said, 'Monet is only an eye. But what an eye!' For the Impressionist painter the transient moment, the impact of light, was of prime importance. In recording ballet and dancers Edgar Degas accepted the Impressionist ideal of trying to seize the instant, but for him this meant an attempt to catch the immediacy of movement seen in the bodies of the dancers of the Paris Opéra. Lillian Browse observes in her masterly *Degas Dancers* (London 1949): 'The dancers had come into their own. Degas had discovered another art through the exploration of which his own was to find fulfilment. No other field allowed such unlimited possibilities of form in movement, a fact which he himself admitted by his relatively small series of Horses, Blanchisseuses and Modistes . . . It must be emphasised how inevitable was his choice, for dancing is the fundamental expression of the human body, and the human body the fundamental form in European art.'

Degas' obsession with the dancer began in the 1870s in the first days of the Third Republic. The Paris Opéra was no longer of any real importance in the world of ballet – that position was to be occupied by the ballet in St Petersburg – but Degas was not interested in ballet as such. He was concerned with the dancers as bodies. As E. H. Gombrich observes, 'He was not interested in the ballerinas because they were pretty girls. He did not seem to care for their moods. He looked at them with the same dispassionate objectivity with which the Impressionists looked at the landscape around them. What mattered to him was the interplay of light and shade on the human form, and the way in which he could suggest movement or space. He proved to the academic world that, far from being incompatible with perfect draughtsmanship, the new principles of the young artists were posing new problems which only the most consummate master of design could solve.'

Here came a vital break in the representation of the dancer by artists. Previously painting, lithography and sculpture were concerned with personality, or with idealising the figure. The dancers were essentially individuals with whom the public might be thought to identify – and later, more indifferent artists, such as

86 Edgar Degas, *Danseuse à la barre*. Pastel and crayon. The image of the dancer stretching and limbering at the *barre* recurs through the entire corpus of Degas' paintings of the dance. The daily labours of class, the basis of the ballet dancer's whole existence, inevitably attracted Degas' attention. In it he could see most clearly the bodily mechanics which so fascinated him. His drawings and sketches of class work show how complete was his understanding of the reality of the dancer's body.

87 Edgar Degas, *Before the Performance*. Oil, c. 1882. Against an unidentified background the dancers are seen in archetypal poses, fiddling with shoes and preparing themselves during those nervous moments before the curtain goes up. The richness of the colouring conveys the intense lighting that obtains on stage before curtain rise.

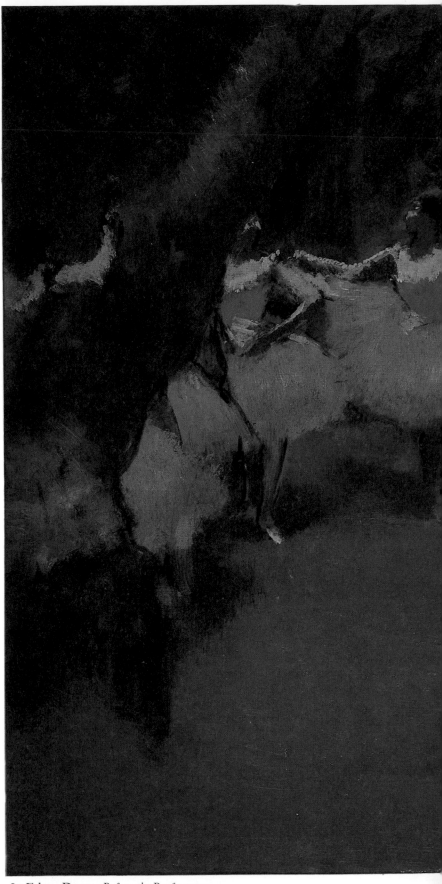

87 Edgar Degas, *Before the Performance*

88 Honoré Daumier, *La Danseuse*. Drawing. Daumier's massive output of lithographs is a resolutely honest and sometimes very bitter view of the France of the middle years of the nineteenth century. This drawing of the dancer is a record of action seized at the very minute – the quick pencil line is eager to catch the flurry of movement as the *danseuse* flutters her skirts.

Clairin, Forain, Bertier and Laurent-Desrousseaux, reverted to this cult. For Degas the dancers served chiefly as abstractions in which movement could be observed at its most refined and disciplined. He was plainly fascinated by the rules of the classic academic dance. The exploration of these rules by the dancer finds its parallel in Degas' reliance upon the rules of draughtsmanship. Any representation of a dancer which does not understand the vital disciplines of turn out, of positions of the feet, of the hard won evolution of the classic technique, all implicit in the dancer's body, must inevitably fail. The average run of depictions of dancers in posters, book illustrations and ephemera always betrays lack of this knowledge. The dancers are not dancers. But Degas – the supreme, the only artist really to have penetrated to the centre of the dancer's art – understood that the academic dance training radically alters the human body. In action the dancer's body 'speaks' differently from those of ordinary people and it is this which Degas shows us.

Other major painters of the period represented dancers merely as decorative figures. Manet's *Lola de Valence* which dates from 1861–62 is a portrait of a Spanish *danseuse* who performed at the Hippodrome in Paris. It is as ravishing in its way as Gainsborough's *Baccelli* – Baudelaire spoke of its 'unexpected charm as of a pink and black jewel' – but it says nothing about dancing.

No less delightful is Renoir's portrait of Rosita Mauri, the Spanish ballerina who was the darling of the Paris Opéra in the 1880s, but again it is a painting of an image seen from the outside rather than an observation based on acute understanding, such as Degas', of the dancer's physique. As a disciple of Degas, Toulouse-Lautrec brought a more sardonic eye to the depiction of all forms of dance. Chiefly concerned with the music hall, the café and the circus, in which he catches everything of the vivacity and sometimes grotesqueness of the popular performers, Toulouse-Lautrec made a few portraits of ballet dancers. In them we see his debt to Degas in the apparently accidental composition – the dancer caught as in a flash of observation.

By the end of the century and in the golden years of the Belle Époque the ballerina had become a symbol of all that was most lavish and worldly. The most celebrated of the *grandes horizontales* were titularly dancers, but such ravishing beauties as Cléo de Mérode and La Belle Otéro owed their fame more to their jewels and extravagance than to their art. The paintings, the postcards and posters which reflected their notoriety also reflected their beauty: as dancers they were hymned as lovely women. Ballet became merely the prettified excuse for the painting, rather than its inspiration.

Ballet itself was now completely moribund in the West, a dainty adjunct to opera performances, in which male roles were usually assigned to pretty girls; Degas never once included a male dancer in his work. It was not until the arrival of the Russian dancers from St Petersburg and Moscow in the first *Saison Russe* organised by Serge Diaghilev in Paris in 1909 that the West was to realise that ballet as an art was alive.

89 Edgar Degas, *Ballet dancer and studies of feet*

90 Edgar Degas, *La Grande Arabesque*

89 Edgar Degas, *Ballet dancer and studies of feet*. Chalk and crayon, 1878–80. In this drawing and its attendant studies of feet Degas demonstrates his interest in the mechanics of the foot in a turned-out position and the dancer's pose as she works on her *pointe*. The drawings show complete understanding of feet properly balanced in the turned-out position, which is the basis of classical ballet.

90 Edgar Degas, *La Grande Arabesque*. Bronze. Degas produced some seventy bronzes which seem both an extension and a commentary on his paintings and drawings of dancers. The most celebrated of these is *La Petite Danseuse de Quatorze Ans* which dates from 1880. During the following decade he also produced the series of studies of naked dancers in various academic positions. *La Grande Arabesque* embodies both the flow of movement and the careful balancing of weight that is an essential part of the arabesque itself.

91 Edgar Degas, *Eugénie Fiocre in 'La Source'*

92 Edgar Degas, *Dancers Resting*

91 Edgar Degas, *Eugénie Fiocre in 'La Source'*. Oil, 1866–67. This is probably the most static of all Degas' paintings of the dance and it is also only his second theatrical work. The ravishing Eugénie Fiocre appeared in Arthur Saint Léon's *La Source* when it was first produced at the Paris Opéra in 1866. The scene Degas recalls is the moment in the first act when the beautiful Nouredda (Fiocre) pauses by a stream. Degas has elaborated this incident by showing Fiocre paddling her feet in the water while her discarded shoes can be seen between the forelegs of a horse. The lack of animation in the painting and in the poses of the dancers was something Degas was soon to abandon.

92 Edgar Degas, *Dancers Resting*. Pastel, 1888–90. Degas found dancers as attractive in repose as in action. These four girls are caught in a shaft of light from a window and their preoccupation with shoes and the fan which one of them holds suggests a moment's break from a rehearsal.

93 Henri de Toulouse-Lautrec, *Dancer adjusting her costume*. Toulouse-Lautrec's world of *café concerts*, bars, brothels and music halls inevitably included dancers. But not for him the fustiness and ritual associated with the Paris Opéra. It was the popular world which fascinated him and his favourite dancing subjects were the figures at the Moulin Rouge, or Jane Avril, or Loie Fuller. There exist several Toulouse-Lautrec drawings showing dancers preparing for performance and adjusting their costumes as in this simple sketch 'after nature'.

94 P. Renouard, *Le Harpiste*. One of a series of engravings of scenes in the Paris Opéra.

95 Jean-Louis Forain, *Dancer and Patron*. Gouache over pencil sketch. Forain's interest in the social identity of the dancer is nowhere better caught than in this brilliant sketch whose subject is entirely self-explanatory. As in Degas' *Dancers Resting*, on the previous page, the backstage activities of the dancers have supplanted their more public image. Their double existence as performers both on and off stage has now entered the accepted canons of representation.

96 H. A. L. Laurent-Desrousseaux, *La Classe de Mme Théodore*. Oil, 1894. This representation of the classroom could not be more different than that provided by Degas. It is a view in which the reality of the dance class is reasonably conveyed, but which also capitalises on the pretty forms of the *danseuses*. Certain facts implied in the picture are of interest: the girls wear the obligatory bloomers which were supposed to maintain standards of decency; the accompaniment is still provided by a violin (the piano was not used in ballet classes until the turn of the century) and the girls at rest are preserving the freshness of their tarlatans by keeping the top layer of the skirt raised. It is, nonetheless, chocolate box art.

93 Henri de Toulouse-Lautrec, *Dancer adjusting her costume*

94 P. Renouard, *Le Harpiste*

95 Jean-Louis Forain, *Dancer and Patron*

96 H. A. L. Laurent-Desrousseaux, *La Classe de Mme Théodore*

97 Pierre Auguste Renoir, *The Young Dancer*. Oil. Renoir's delight in this young dancer is evident. The tenderness and warmth with which the girl is caught in a balletic stance (her feet are sketching a third position) suggest an idealisation of the *rat de l'Opéra*. But she is less a dancer than a very pretty girl in a ballet costume.

98 Edgar Degas, *The Ballet Scene from 'Robert le Diable'*. Oil, 1876. The informality with which Degas shows the figures in the audience and in the orchestra reflects his concern with light, and the dancing figures of the nuns, in the ballet scene from Meyerbeer's opera, are secondary to the heads in the foreground. See also plate 56.

99 Edgar Degas, *The Dance Class of Monsieur Perrot*. Oil, 1873–74. Of the several studies which Degas did of dancers in class, two are of particular interest for the ballet lover. Both produced in the early 1870s and both similar in structure, they show the venerable figure of Jules Perrot as teacher. This greatest choreographer of the Romantic period was no longer producing ballets; instead, he was passing on the dance traditions which he had inherited from his master Auguste Vestris. This version of the class catches a moment of repose as Perrot gestures to the dancer in front of him in explanation.

97 Pierre Auguste Renoir, *The Young Dancer*

98 Edgar Degas, *The Ballet Scene from 'Robert le Diable'*

99 Edgar Degas, *The Dance Class of Monsieur Perrot*

100 E. Debat-Ponsan, *La Maladetta*. 1893. *La Maladetta*, a ballet with choreography by Joseph Hansen and music by Paul Vidal, was first staged at the Paris Opéra in 1893. It starred Rosita Mauri, whose beauty and allure are admirably caught in this painting. It offers interesting testimony to the warmth of Mauri's personality: born in Spain, she excelled in roles which allowed her temperament full reign. Debat-Ponsan is plainly inspired by Mauri, and his painting does her far greater justice, as a portrait and as the record of an individual dancer, than was usual at the turn of the century.

101 Georges Clairin, *Virginia Zucchi*. Oil, 1884. Virginia Zucchi is one of the most exceptional of the virtuoso ballerinas who dominated dance at the end of the nineteenth century. Possessed of genius as a dramatic performer, her appearances in St Petersburg in the 1880s were responsible for the renewal of Russian interest in ballet at this time. At the Eden Theatre, Paris (a hall given over to musical extravaganzas), the Italian choreographer Manzotti staged a series of spectacles. Among them, *Siéba* featured Zucchi, and Clairin's portrait offers a slightly provocative view of a great dancer. She was far more serious an artist, and more important a performer, than this obviously alluring and essentially cheap representation suggests.

102 Nicolas and Serge Legat, *Marie M. Petipa*. Coloured lithograph. The Legat brothers were among the most brilliant male dancers of the Imperial Ballet in St Petersburg at the beginning of the twentieth century. Among their hobbies was that of caricature, in which they jointly excelled, and an album of some one hundred of these caricatures was produced in St Petersburg in 1900. The drawings mocked none too gently the foibles and qualities of the Legats' colleagues. The portrait of Marie Mariusovna Petipa, daughter of the great ballet master, shows her in *Paquita*, in ballet's idea of Spanish costume. It also celebrates a certain generosity of *embonpoint* and her affection for 'important' jewels – which were then sported by dancers on stage.

100 E. Debat-Ponsan, *La Maladetta*

101 Georges Clarin, *Virginia Zucchi*

102 Nicolas and Serge Legat, *Marie M. Petipa*

Pages 86–87

103 Jean-Louis Forain, *Danseuse*. Oil. Although he is more generally known as a master of etching and lithography, Forain also produced a series of paintings in which his concern with the immediate event was quite as brilliant as that of his friend and patron, Degas. Like Degas, he was fascinated by the world of the theatre, but his interest was not so much with the capturing of movement as with the social and moral identity of the dancer. The *danseuse* in plate 103 is pictured in the wings of the theatre and her dress suggests involvement in some pseudo-Spanish enterprise.

104 Jean Béraud, *Les Coulisses de l'Opéra*. Oil, 1889. Nothing more accurately conveys the state of ballet as an art at the end of the nineteenth century than this piece of reportage by Béraud. By now ballet and the ballet dancer had become totally debased in the public imagination. The *corps de ballet* of the Paris Opéra was a collection of young women as marketable as any other commodity. The cohorts of admirers who are seen in attentive poses are all too obviously concerned with life rather than art. It seems almost by accident that one of the girls is shown in a balletic pose. The excuse for their appearance is the obligatory ballet scene that was interpolated into every opera and interpolated late enough to allow the gentlemen of the Jockey Club to dine before coming in for the ballet scene and then leave to organize an intimate supper with the lady of their choice.

105 Henri de Toulouse-Lautrec, *Loie Fuller*. Sketch for a poster, 1893. The effect of Loie Fuller in Paris was instantaneous: her dances, by the swirling shapes created with skirts and draperies, were a realisation of the sinuous lines of *art nouveau*. In making his lithographic posters of her, Lautrec was at pains to ink his stones with several colours to capture the varying shades of La Loie's draperies on each impression, subsequently sprinkling them with gold dust. This first sketch exactly suggests the convolutions of La Loie's veil dancing.

103 Jean-Louis Forain, *Danseuse*

104 Jean Béraud, *Les Coulisses de l'Opéra*

105 Henri de Toulouse-Lautrec, *Loie Fuller*

THE DIAGHILEV YEARS

If it can be said at all that one man took ballet from the thin aristocratic stratum of society and gave it to the people at large, Diaghilev was the man who did it.

George Balanchine

The twenty years of the Diaghilev enterprise (1909–29) saw the life span of what is generally acknowledged as the single greatest artistic enterprise of this century. It is testimony to the stature of Diaghilev himself that at his death at the age of 57, in 1929, the Ballet Russe could no longer continue. The Ballet Russe was, though, only the culminating achievement of this exceptional man, who laboured long to serve the arts of his native Russia before his decision in 1906 to bring exhibitions of painting, then concerts, then operas and finally ballets to Paris, to reveal to the West the vitality of the arts in his homeland.

As a young man of good family Sergey Diaghilev had studied law, but his great love was music. When, in a brisk interview with Rimsky-Korsakov, he was disabused of his ambitions as a composer, he turned his phenomenal energies to a career as a promoter of painting. In this he was guided, and his taste encouraged, by two artists – Alexandre Benois and Léon Bakst – who remained central to his achievements for many years. The magazine *The World of Art*, which Diaghilev directed for ten years at the turn of the century, was vital in awakening Russian taste to what was new in art, and the exhibitions which he organised to show European painting in Russia were symptomatic of the growing awareness there of the newest currents in Western art.

Wealthy Muscovite collectors were among the first important patrons of the Fauve painters; the patronage of the millionaire industrialist Savva Mamontov brought such important Russian artists as Korovin and Golovin into the theatre as decorators for his private operatic performances. It is not unreasonable to assume that Diaghilev and his associates learnt from Mamontov's example, and when Diaghilev organised the first Russian season of opera in Paris in 1908 the decorative splendour of the works presented contributed greatly to their success.

Diaghilev's constant quest for the new made him the great explorer of ways in which painting could serve to enhance theatrical spectacle. It is to Diaghilev's example that we owe the

106 Jean Cocteau, *Nijinsky in 'Le Spectre de la Rose'*. Poster, 1911. Cocteau's poster, showing Nijinsky as the Rose, is a stylised and clever piece of draughtsmanship.

107 Léon Bakst, *Nijinsky as the Faun*

108 Léon Bakst, Design for a Bacchante in *Narcisse*

107 Léon Bakst, *Nijinsky as the Faun*. Watercolour, 1912. Bakst's Hellenism produced some magnificent stage décors – *Daphnis and Chloe*, *Hélène de Sparte*, *Narcisse*, *L'après-midi d'un faune* – as well as the painting *Terror Antiquus*. His design for Nijinsky as the Faun is far more than a mere working drawing: it is a telling portrait of the dancer as the character and also a masterly piece of decoration.

108 Léon Bakst, Design for a Bacchante in *Narcisse*. Watercolour, 1911. Although this is costume design for a Fokine ballet staged by Diaghilev in 1911, it is design raised to the level of high art. The eroticism of the girl's clothes and the sensuality with which Bakst has treated her body and its draperies are an extraordinary tribute to Bakst's power as a painter.

109 Léon Bakst, *Nijinsky in 'La Péri'*. Watercolour, 1911. Diaghilev had hoped to stage *La Péri*, the *poème dansée* by Paul Dukas, but in the event it was acquired by the indifferent dancer Natalia Trouhanova through her friendship with the composer. Nevertheless, Bakst had begun work on designs for the ballet and this portrait of Nijinsky in costume is both a design and an evocation.

109 Léon Bakst, *Nijinsky in 'La Péri'*

110 Émile-Antoine Bourdelle, *Nijinsky as Harlequin in 'Le Carnaval'*. Drawing. Bourdelle's drawing pinpoints the quality of malicious delight which is the essence of this role.

rebirth of ballet in the West, and his involvement of many of the greatest painters of the century as decorators means that the décors for ballets produced under his banner often survive as works of art in their own right. It suffices to list the painters employed by Diaghilev – some of them producing their first theatre work for him – to indicate the stature of design in the Ballet Russe. Diaghilev's Ballet Russe was in fact a travelling exhibition of the works of the following artists: Benois, Bakst, Korovin, Roerich, Golovin, Anisfeld, Sudeikin, Dobuzhinsky, Sert, Goncharova, Larionov, Balla, Picasso, Matisse, Derain, Gris, Laurencin, Braque, Laurens, Pruna, Utrillo, Ernst, Miró, Gabo, Pevsner, Yakulov, Tchelitchev, Bauchant, de Chirico, Rouault.

Vital to the understanding of Diaghilev's work is the fact that after the 1917 Revolution he and his ballet were émigrés. Moreover, while beginning as a Russian company, feeding on the greatest traditions of Russian art and music, Diaghilev's quest for the new brought him into contact with Parisian taste and with the artistic apparatus of the École de Paris. Furthermore, where he had been in the avant-garde before the Revolution, the last decade of his company's existence found him obliged to seek the new wherever he could find it, in an endeavour to keep up with his pre-war reputation. The undeniable chic of the company during the 1920s is reflected in such airy delights as *Les Biches*. The sometime desperate quest for novelty can be noted in the pseudo-Soviet disaster *Le Pas d'acier*, which provided salon communism for the Train Bleu audience (and the Train Bleu itself offered the excuse for an 'amusing' work by Jean Cocteau).

But whatever the straining after novel pleasures to delight a worldly audience, the solid basis of the repertory and the superlative standards of presentation remained. Throughout the entire twenty years of the Diaghilev Ballet it never ceased to attract and fascinate the foremost artists of the time. As collaborators with Diaghilev they became involved not only in designing works but also in the daily life of the company. And there results from this close communion a very rich gallery of portraits which celebrate the beauty of the dancers and the vitality of the company's creative ambience.

Ephemeral, but very pertinent, are the innumerable caricatures which survive as testimony to the daily activities of the collaborators. Mikhail Larionov was constantly drawing Diaghilev and his entourage – the last portrait we have of Diaghilev shows him in bed in the Grand Hotel, Paris in 1929, correcting a score. Benois could sketch Ravel standing on the beach at St Jean de Luz. Picasso, at the time of his collaboration on *Parade*, caught Massine, Diaghilev and Bakst sitting outside a café in Rome. Stravinsky caricatured Bakst. Bakst produced a magnificent head of Diaghilev on the writing paper of the Branksome Hotel, Bournemouth. Jean Cocteau was indefatigable in caricaturing everyone: Poulenc at the piano, Nijinsky in rehearsal, Stravinsky pounding out the rhythms of *Le Sacre du Printemps*, Stravinsky watching Nijinsky making up for *Le Carnaval*, Diaghilev as the Young Girl in *Spectre de la Rose* and Bakst as the Rose.

Once he was drawn into the world of the Ballet Russe, Pablo Picasso discovered a source of inspiration which was to last him until the end of his life. Quite apart from his theatre work, which extended to his redesigning of Serge Lifar's *Icare* in 1962, Picasso became even more intimate with the ballet through his meeting with a Ballet Russe dancer, Olga Khokhlova, in 1916 and their marriage a year later. His drawings of dancers which date from this period are marked by an almost classical approach in draughtsmanship. Such works as the portrait of Olga in Spanish costume and the depiction of three male dancers resting, from as late as 1925, are beautifully serene in execution. Like Degas before him, Picasso demonstrates that essential understanding of the dancers' physiques: his dancers are truly dancers. But Picasso also fed upon dancing to find his inspiration in very different ways, most significantly in the tremendous *Three Dancers*, also dating from 1925, a work which shows a significant change in his style, and whose ferocity and emotional violence mark it as one of his major creations. The figures are not recognisably classical ballet dancers, but they reaffirm Picasso's fascination with dance in his determination to show many facets of the human figure at the same time.

In 1954, to commemorate the twenty-fifth anniversary of Diaghilev's death, the ballet critic Richard Buckle organised a fine Diaghilev exhibition, seen first at the Edinburgh Festival and then in an enlarged form at Forbes House in London. The shade of Diaghilev himself seemed to pervade the enterprise. Buckle worked in the Diaghilev tradition, finding a new and creative way of displaying exhibits so that the actual life of the Ballet Russe could be sensed. The richness of the Ballet Russe activity was evident from the range and multiplicity of objects on display. The Ballet Russe itself, as well as the works it created, had offered constant inspiration to artists, as was evident from the extraordinary wealth of portraiture. In one gallery were portraits of the stars, collaborators and patrons of the Diaghilev Ballet, and it was possible to see nine different views of Tamara Karsavina, seven of Serge Lifar, six of Lydia Lopokova, seven of Leonid Massine and thirteen of Nijinsky. In his book about the exhibition, *In Search of Diaghilev* (London 1955) Buckle records how he had to resort to guile to obtain some of the material. Leonid Massine had failed to answer several requests for items from his collection. Buckle wrote a final plea: 'You must admit that it will be absurd if there are eight portraits of Lifar in the exhibition, and none of you.' Massine's reply then came by return of post: 'If you will guarantee to pay the costs of transport and insure the pictures for $1,000 each . . . I will order to be released for you one portrait of me by Bakst, one by Derain, one by Matisse, three by Picasso . . .'

The entire history of the Diaghilev Ballet can be traced both in portraiture and in caricature. Stravinsky noted that immediately after the first performance of *The Firebird* in Paris in 1910 Jacques-Émile Blanche, 'a *fine mouche* for a celebrity', came to make his portrait. The impact of Karsavina and Nijinsky can be found in the admirable drawings made by John Singer Sargent at the behest of Lady Ripon, an early patron of Diaghilev, and in their portraits by

111 Ludwig Kainer, *Karsavina in 'Le Dieu Bleu'*. Drawing, 1912. *Le Dieu Bleu* was a confection devised by Cocteau and Reynaldo Hahn, most charming of composers, to satisfy a continuing public demand for oriental fantasy in the manner of *Schéhérazade*. The ballet was not a success, despite the opulence of Bakst's designs, but Kainer's drawing – one of many he made of the Ballet Russe – does convey something of Karsavina's presence, playing a Young Girl who tries to stop her beloved from becoming a Hindu priest.

112 Spencer Frederick Gore, *Our Flag*. Oil, 1910. The English painter Spencer Frederick Gore was influenced both by the manner of Sickert and by late Impressionist painting. Like Sickert he was attracted to the theatre and in the early 1900s he made records of the ballet performances at the Alhambra and Empire Theatres in London. His view of *Our Flag* shows the Danish ballerina Britta as the Spirit of the Flag in one of the patriotic works which typified the miserable state of ballet in London before the arrival of Diaghilev. Spencer Gore catches everything of its hectic and inartistic manner.

113 Everett Shinn, *Ballet in the Park*. Oil. Everett Shinn was a member of that group of American painters at the turn of the twentieth century who sought a style of painting which was consonant with American life. Called 'The Ash Can School' because of their recognition of the importance of everyday subjects for art, many had begun working as illustrators for newspapers in the 1890s, making drawings of events to accompany press reports. In the days before photography was universally used in newspapers they developed a quick, almost shorthand style of recording. One of the leaders of the Ash Can School, Robert Henri, urged his colleagues to adopt this quickness of style in their paintings. Shinn demonstrates this skill in catching effects of light but for him, as for many other artists, painting was still essentially European and conservative, never totally accepting the socialism implicit in the Ash Can School's ideas. During the first few decades of the twentieth century, Shinn became attracted to the style of Degas and this painting of an open air ballet performance records an elegant audience watching a performance of *Les Sylphides*. The pose of the dancers is reminiscent of a celebrated early photograph of *Les Sylphides* in Paris in 1909.

112 Spencer Frederick Gore, *Our Flag*

113 Everett Shinn, *Ballet in the Park*

114 Natalia Goncharova, *Les Noces*. Pen and ink, 1923. With music by Igor Stravinsky, choreography by Bronislava Nijinska and designs by Natalia Goncharova, *Les Noces* was an evocation of the peasant faith of Holy Russia. Nijinska's dances were conceived in monolithic architectural terms. This drawing is one of several that Goncharova made: it shows the bridesmaids holding the long ritualistic braids of the bride and it indicates one of the pyramidal groupings of the choreography.

Blanche. In the latter years of the company the young English artist Christopher Wood, who became involved with the Diaghilev enterprise in 1926, produced some entertaining caricatures and portraits.

Contemporary with Diaghilev, two great stars reflect the extreme poles of the dancer's art: Anna Pavlova and Isadora Duncan. Pavlova, briefly associated with Diaghilev in his first seasons, went off to pursue a career of her own. The records of her genius are few: the multitudinous portraits offer likenesses but not insight. Valerian Svetlov's biography (Paris 1922) is crowded with tasteless illustrations of her impact on the world. There are few representations of her which do anything like justice to her incomparable artistry.

Very different was the case of Isadora Duncan. Edward Gordon Craig, in a BBC broadcast in 1952, best summed up the impact that Duncan had upon those who watched her. 'Was it art? No, it was not. It was something which inspires those men who labour in the narrower fields of the arts, harder but more lasting. It released the minds of hundreds of such men: one had but to see her dance for one's thoughts to wing their way, as it were, with the fresh air. It rid us of all nonsense we had been pondering so long. How is that – for she said nothing? On the contrary, she said everything that was worth hearing; and everything that anyone else but the poets had forgotten to say.' Thus it is that we find Isadora recorded not only by Craig, who loved her, but also by Bourdelle who immortalised her in the reliefs he made for the Théâtre des Champs Elysées in 1913, by Bakst, by Carrière, by Rodin and Jose Clara, by Segonzac and many more.

In each representation, the passionate life of her art can be perceived. Isadora the revolutionary attracted the more adventurous artists; Pavlova's conservatism of taste – which had alienated her from Diaghilev – is reflected in the many conventional portrayals which minimise her genius. But it is to Pavlova that we turn in gratitude as the greater propagandist for ballet itself. She had started to travel at the beginning of the century, while still a member of the Imperial Russian Ballet, and from 1913 her journeyings were worldwide and ceaseless. She took ballet where it had never been seen before; her image is the popular one of the ballerina. She instilled a love and a feeling for ballet in generations of admirers.

By taking ballet away from the institutionalised setting of the opera house, Diaghilev and Pavlova were responsible for the first increase in its popularity in the present century. But there is nothing in the visual arts that reflects this popularity as did the lithographs and prints that proliferated during the last high point of public interest in ballet during the Romantic era. Dance now seems to lie in the realm of the still and moving camera. It is tragic to recall that there exists not one minute of film of the Diaghilev Ballet or of its great stars, and that Anna Pavlova is known to us only through ultimately unsatisfactory fragments. At a time when artists were seeking new ways of revealing the world around them, and nineteenth-century representationalism had been left to the academies, the camera remained to record the dancer's art.

115 Léon Bakst, Design for *Le Festin (L'Oiseau d'or)*.
Used as a cover for the number of the magazine
Commoedia Illustré which commemorated the first
Russian season of the Ballet Russe in 1909.

116 Georges Barbier, *Nijinsky and Ida Rubinstein in 'Schéhérazade'*

Vaslav Nijinsky

Nijinsky remains the most celebrated male dancer of
this century. At a time when male dancing had fallen
into the worst disrepute in Western Europe,
Nijinsky's genius – combining phenomenal
technique and no less phenomenal dramatic power –
reasserted the importance of men in ballet. His
tragically short career as a performer lasted only ten
years before the clouds of mental illness cut him off
from the world in 1917. But from 1909, when he
first appeared in Paris, until 1913, when he broke
with Diaghilev, he proved an irresistible figure to
artists of all kinds. From the many works inspired by
him, the following six convey his range, his animal
attraction and his magnetism, evident even in
indifferent portrayals of him.

John Singer Sargent made a drawing (117) which
fixes for us the allure and radiant beauty of the
young Nijinsky as he appeared in *Le Pavillon
d'Armide*. It catches particularly the extraordinary
placing of Nijinsky's head on his neck and the
vitality of presence which was Nijinsky's once he
had put on a costume.

Georges Barbier's view of Nijinsky and Ida
Rubinstein in *Schéhérazade* (116) is Beardsleyesque in
its manipulation of black and white and it indicates
how strongly Parisian taste had been caught by the
exoticism of Bakst's designs.

In 1912 Jean Cocteau – a member of the
Diaghilev entourage from the first *Saison Russe* –
made one of his many caricatures (118) showing
Nijinsky in the wings ready to go on as the Golden
Slave in *Schéhérazade*, with behind him the dominat-
ing figure of Diaghilev. Diaghilev's features are
exactly as Cocteau has recorded them in his prose:
'Eyes like Portuguese oysters and baby crocodile's
teeth'.

117 John Singer Sargent, *Nijinsky in 'Le Pavillon d'Armide'*

118 Jean Cocteau, Nijinsky and Diaghilev

99

Nijinsky (continued)

In the first season in Paris of the Russian dancers, Nijinsky appeared in the Bluebird *pas de deux* from the last act of *The Sleeping Beauty*. It formed part of a *divertissement* called *Le Festin*, and because Diaghilev had announced *The Firebird*, which was not to be created until the following season, Nijinsky was billed as '*l'oiseau d'or*'. Barbier's drawing (119) dates from three years later and is a fantasy upon the Bakst costume. It is one of a series of drawings made for a de luxe edition about Nijinsky published in Paris in 1913, and the pose is almost identical with that in a Barbier drawing of Nijinsky as the Favourite Slave in *Cléopâtre*.

Marc Chagall made a drawing in 1911 (120, Collection of the Museum of Modern Art, New York) in pen and ink and gouache of Nijinsky as the Rose. The Cocteau poster (106) and this drawing testify, as do many others, to the extraordinary impact that this brief duet, for Nijinsky and Karsavina, had upon artists.

In 1912 Nijinsky's first ballet, *L'après-midi d'un faune,* was publicly censured as obscene. Rodin leapt to Nijinsky's defence in a letter to the daily newspaper *Le Matin* and subsequently Nijinsky visited Rodin in his studio and danced for him. A result of this meeting was this bronze (121). Like the other sculptures of dancers made towards the end of Rodin's life, it was an entirely private piece of work – none of the dancing figures was cast or shown until after his death. They represent a final summation of his genius.

119 Georges Barbier, *Nijinsky in 'Le Festin'*

120 Marc Chagall, *Nijinsky in 'Le Spectre de la Rose'*

121 Auguste Rodin, *Nijinsky*

122 John Singer Sargent, *Karsavina in 'Le Dieu Bleu'*

123 Jacques-Émile Blanche, *Karsavina as The Firebird*

124 Paul Scheurich, *Karsavina and Nijinsky in 'Le Carnaval'*

125 Glyn Philpot, *Karsavina as Thamar*

126 Jean Cocteau, Poster for the Ballet Russe

Tamara Karsavina

Most loved of Diaghilev's ballerinas, Karsavina was a product of the Imperial Ballet School in St Petersburg. It was she, though, who best understood the ideals of the new ballet as propounded by Fokine and Diaghilev, and she was the female star of the Diaghilev seasons until the First World War. After a return to Russia, she married an English diplomat, H. J. Bruce, and settled in England, where her presence was an inspiration to everyone connected with ballet. Great artists of almost every European nationality created portraits of her: in her most famous roles, in her dressing room, in society. She was depicted in oils and watercolours, drawings, engravings, statuettes of porcelain, silver and bronze.

John Singer Sargent was plainly fascinated by Karsavina's beauty, notably the lustrous eyes which gave such expression to her performances. The head from *Le Dieu Bleu* (122), drawn in charcoal, tells us everything of the languorous grace of her interpretation.

Jacques-Émile Blanche was one of the most fashionable portraitists of his time and with the advent of the Diaghilev Russian seasons Blanche (whom Stravinsky observed had 'a keen nose for a celebrity') was quick to engage in a series of portraits of the most distinguished artists in the Russian Ballet. Karsavina is shown (123) in the pose the Firebird adopts in the Lullaby of the second scene, standing in front of a coromandel screen in Blanche's studio. The portrait is entirely faithful in capturing the beauty of the model and the exotic brilliance of the costume designed by Léon Bakst.

The popularity of the Ballet Russe also brought a revival in the manufacture of good porcelain models of dancers. The Meissen factory commissioned the artist Paul Scheurich to model a complete set of the characters in Fokine's ballet, *Le Carnaval*. The pair illustrated (124) shows Karsavina and Nijinsky as Columbine and Harlequin. The quality of these Meissen figures maintains the great tradition of modelling in this medium, a tradition which was to become appallingly debased in later years. Today, porcelain models of dancers are almost always masterpieces of kitsch in which vulgarity and physical improbability horridly combine.

Glyn Philpot was fascinated by Karsavina's appearance as Thamar. His brilliant study in oils (125) catches the ruthlessness of the Queen as she poses watchfully on the piled cushions which featured in the amazing Bakst design.

As a companion piece to his posters of Pavlova and Nijinsky, Jean Cocteau made delightful capital out of the figure of Karsavina as the Young Girl in *Le Spectre de la Rose* (126). Eyes shut, she seems to be dreaming of the ball.

127 André Dunoyer de Segonzac, *Fokine and Karsavina in 'Le Carnaval'*

128 Valentin Serov, *Portrait of Karsavina*

Karsavina (continued)

André Dunoyer de Segonzac produced a number of quick, almost calligraphic impressions of dancers, and this view (127) of Fokine and Karsavina is taken on the wing. No more than a caricature, it nonetheless captures the mischievous nature of the characters in *Le Carnaval*.

Valentin Serov's pencil drawing of Karsavina (128) dates from her early years in St Petersburg. With extreme simplicity it reveals the freshness of her beauty and the exquisite quality of her profile: no wonder the entire student population of St Petersburg was in love with her. Serov, a pupil of Repin, was a precociously brilliant draughtsman and around the turn of the century he became the most accomplished and successful portraitist in Russia.

Charles Hallo's affection for views from the wings of the Paris Opéra produced this atmospheric glimpse of Karsavina in performance as the Firebird (129).

129 Charles Hallo, *The Firebird*

Anna Pavlova

Sir John Lavery, one of the most successful and
honoured painters of his time, made three fine
studies of Anna Pavlova. *The Dying Swan* (131) was
Pavlova's most celebrated solo, and Lavery offers an
interpretation of her in this role. Pavlova's position
is not one found in her dance and it seems as if
Lavery has shown her in the grounds of her North
London home, Ivy House, where the ballerina was
much given to posing with her pet swan by the lake.
The Pavlova in *Autumn Bacchanale* (130), with the
grapes and vineleaves framing the beautiful face, is
Pavlova the ballerina, the *assoluta* with the world at
her feet.

  Léon Bakst was a masterly portraitist and his
drawings of members of the Diaghilev entourage are
well known. The drawing of Pavlova (132) is a
product of his last years and it reflects his deep
understanding of his subject, whom he had known
since her début in St Petersburg in 1899. In this
drawing Bakst seems to have stripped away all the
external glamour of the ballerina image to reveal
something essential about a forty-year-old woman
who is universally acclaimed. It is without question
the best portrait of Pavlova, whose curse it is to
have been celebrated in an infinity of indifferent
works of art.

130 John Lavery, *Pavlova in 'Autumn Bacchanale'*

131 John Lavery, *The Dying Swan*

132 Léon Bakst, *Portrait of Anna Pavlova*

133 Auguste Rodin, *Isadora Duncan*

134, 135 Émile-Antoine Bourdelle, *Isadora Duncan*

133 Auguste Rodin, *Isadora Duncan*. Pencil and wash. In the last two decades of his life Rodin started to make an extraordinary series of drawings of dancers – both the exotics who visited Paris (Javanese dancers in 1896, Cambodian dancers ten years later) and, inevitably, Isadora Duncan. In Anthony Ludovici's *Personal Reminiscences of Auguste Rodin* (Philadelphia, 1926), the artist is quoted as saying, '. . . my drawings are only my way of testing myself. They are my way of proving to myself how far this incorporation of the subtle secrets of the human form has taken place within me. I try to see the figure as a mass, a volume. It is the voluminousness

that I try to understand. That is why, as you see, I sometimes wash a tint over the drawings. This completes the feeling of massiveness, and helps me to ascertain how far I have succeeded in grasping the movement as a mass . . .'

134, 135 Émile-Antoine Bourdelle, *Isadora Duncan*. Pen and ink, 1909. Bourdelle has been attracted by the young Isadora at her most joyous. These drawings convey the quality that was so subtly evoked by Sir Frederick Ashton in his *Isadora Duncan Dances* created for Lynn Seymour in 1976.

Ida Rubinstein

Ida Rubinstein was one of the most mysterious figures in the ballet of the twentieth century. Of a wealthy Moscow family, she was a woman of stunning beauty whose ambitions as a performer were rarely realised on stage. A private pupil of Fokine, she appeared in mime roles during the early Diaghilev Ballet Russe seasons. Her striking appearance compensated for any lack of technique. At various times thereafter she formed companies in which she appeared, and sought to perpetuate her beauty in a variety of specially created roles.

Serov's portrait in oils (137) tells a great deal about the exoticism and glamour of her presence. It is a portrait very consciously arranged in its angular lines, which stress the sudden decorative moments of rings on toes and fingers and the conflicting mass of the russet hair which framed the ravishing face.

Romaine Brooks' etiolated portrait of Rubinstein (136) is sometimes known as *la femme morte*. It is a macabre view of its subject, painted in oils in 1911, owing something to the decadent art of the Symbolists. It suggests, though, the extraordinary attraction that Rubinstein had for her admirers.

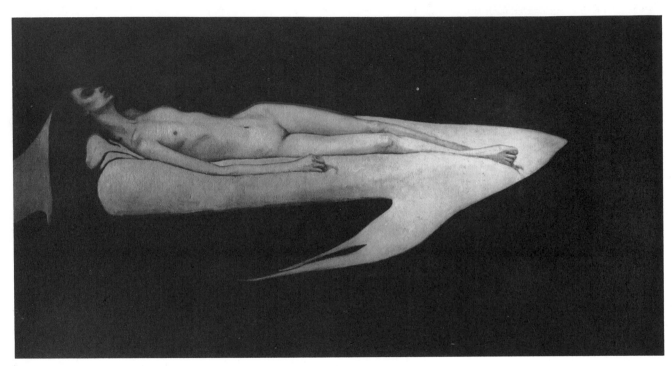

136 Romaine Brooks, *Le Trajet*

137 Valentin Serov, *Ida Rubinstein*

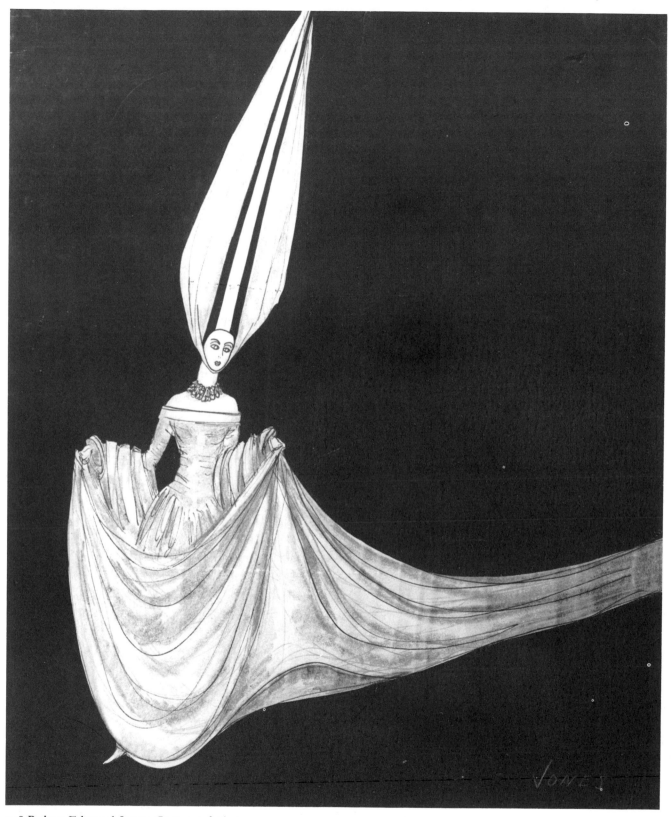

138 Robert Edmond Jones, Costume design

138 Robert Edmond Jones, Design for a Chateleine in *Tyl Eulenspiegel*. This ballet was staged by the Diaghilev Ballet Russe in New York in 1916 with choreography by Nijinsky.

139 Pablo Picasso, *Four Dancers*

139 Pablo Picasso, *Four Dancers*. Pen and ink, 1925.
Museum of Modern Art, New York.

140 Pablo Picasso, *La Boutique fantasque*. Pen and
sepia ink, 1919. In 1919 one of Leonid Massine's
most enduring and delightful ballets was given its
first performance in London. Picasso's page of quick
sketches is a souvenir of a time when he was in
London with the Ballet Russe for the staging of *Le
Tricorne* which he had designed and which had its
first performance in London on July 22, 1919.
Boutique had been given its premiere just two weeks
before. The sketches show Lydia Lopokova and

Massine as the Can-Can dancers. Dedicated by the
artist to Massine, the sketches have a wonderful
immediacy.

141 Pablo Picasso, *Two Dancers*. Ink, 1926.
After his marriage to Olga Khokhlova and his
involvement with first ballet design in 1917, for the
Ballet Russe production of *Parade*, Picasso spent a
decade immersed in the world of the Ballet Russe.
He drew it repeatedly, making a series of brilliant
portraits of the various members of the Diaghilev
entourage and also immersing himself in the physical
attitudes of dancers. Not since Degas had an artist

140 Pablo Picasso, *La Boutique fantasque*

been so obsessed with dance movement. The presence of dancers is found not only in his masterly drawings – which seem to prefer performers in rehearsal rather than in the theatre – but many of the paintings during this decade reflect, by attitudes and arrangements of limbs, the continued fact of the ballet world in Picasso's consciousness. In his definitive *Picasso Theatre* (Weidenfeld & Nicolson, London, 1968) Douglas Cooper observes: 'By 1925 Picasso was tired of his long association with the ballet, his marriage had become a source of irritation to him, he had found new artistic interests and he was determined to free himself from the claims of the theatre. In April of that year Picasso and Olga paid a last visit to Diaghilev and his Ballet Russe at Monte Carlo, where he made drawings of elegantly posed dancers as he had done previously. But when he got back to Paris a month later he painted *The Dance*, a climactic masterpiece in which the elation he had once felt is overlaid with pain and in which dancing and dancers are treated with bitter mockery. This painting was a true cry from the heart, a passionate and spontaneous outburst which marks the end of Picasso's interest in ballet for twenty years.'

141 Pablo Picasso, *Two Dancers*

142 Émile-Antoine Bourdelle, *Isadora Duncan*

142 Émile-Antoine Bourdelle, *Isadora Duncan*. Pen and wash. Isadora Duncan's impact upon European artists can be traced in the innumerable drawings and sculptures which exist of her. Like his master Rodin, Bourdelle was enraptured by her art; he told his students: 'All my muses in the theatre are movements seized during Isadora's flight; she was my principal source'. In his sketches, as in his sculptures, Bourdelle captured both the monumental quality of Isadora's dance and also its Dionysiac abandon. This drawing illustrates a pose expressive of grief: in it we sense, as always with Bourdelle, the actuality of Isadora.

143 Abraham Walkowitz, *Isadora Duncan*. Pen and watercolour. In a series of drawings dating from 1920 Abraham Walkowitz provided eloquent testimony to the grander impulses and more monumental tone of Duncan's dancing in the last, dark decades of her life.

144 Mikhail Larionov, *Soleil de Nuit*. Watercolour, 1915. This impression, by its designer, of Massine's first ballet for Diaghilev shows the peasant vitality which informed the early work of Larionov. He remained one of Diaghilev's closest associates.

143 Abraham Walkowitz, *Isadora Duncan*

144 Mikhail Larionov, *Soleil de Nuit*

145 Mikhail Larionov, *Diaghilev watching Lifar in rehearsal*

145 Mikhail Larionov, *Diaghilev watching Lifar in rehearsal*. Pen and ink, 1927. Larionov's rehearsal drawing says a great deal about the toil of a dancer's life, from the watering can with which the floor is kept damp and unslippery, to the looking glass against which Diaghilev is sitting, and the energetic figures of the dancers at work. Serge Lifar is seated in the foreground.

146 George William Bissill, *Anton Dolin in 'Le Train Bleu'*. Pen, Indian ink and water colour, 1924. *Le Train Bleu* was the quintessential *chic* ballet of the 1920s. With its music by Milhaud, choreography by Nijinska, decor by Laurens and costumes by Chanel, it typified the quest for the 'amusing'. It was inspired by Cocteau seeing Dolin performing hand-stands in Monte Carlo. From this there developed the idea of the ballet which was given its title because, as Diaghilev observed, 'the first point about *Le Train Bleu* is that there is no Blue Train in it'. Bissill's drawing shows Dolin in the acrobatic choreography which became so associated with him at this time.

147 Eileen Mayo, *Serge Lifar in 'La Chatte'*. Pencil and crayon, 1928. *La Chatte*, first produced by Diaghilev's Ballet Russe in Monte Carlo in 1927, was

146 George William Bissill, *Anton Dolin in 'Le Train Bleu'*

an updating of one of Aesop's fables, given a brilliant Constructivist decor and costumes by Naum Gabo and Antoine Pevsner. Eileen Mayo's drawing is a souvenir of the beauty of *le beau Serge* and of the extraordinary lighting effects obtained from the black floorcloth and transparent mica shapes of the setting.

147 Eileen Mayo, *Serge Lifar in 'La Chatte'*

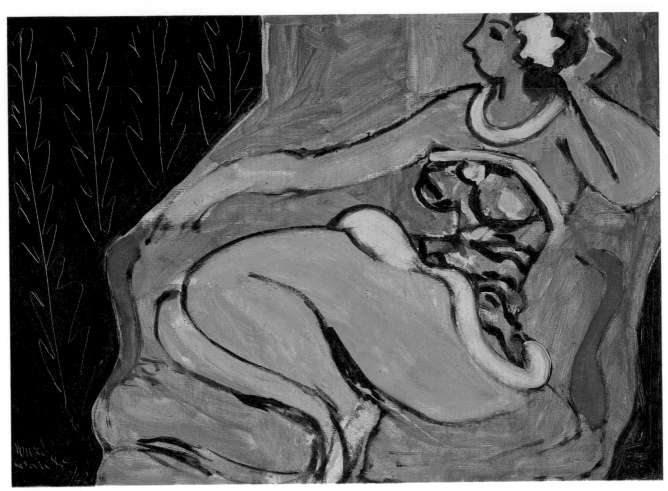

148 Henri Matisse, *Dancer and Armchair, black background*

148 Henri Matisse, *Dancer and Armchair, black background*. Oil, 1942. Matisse's involvement with the ballet started with his designs for *Le Chant du Rossignol* which he made for Diaghilev in 1920. After a later revival of the work in 1925, this exercise in Chinoiserie was his only connection with the ballet until he was invited to design Massine's *Rouge et Noir* in 1939. He turned, instead, to dancers as subjects for painting and during the 1920s and 1930s he celebrated the female form in a sequence of oil paintings of voluptuous beauty. Talking of his work at this time he said, 'I depend entirely on my model whom I observe at liberty, and then I decide on the pose that best suits her nature. When I take a new model I guess the appropriate position from the abandoned attitudes of repose, and then I become the slave of that pose'.

149 Marie Laurencin. *Le Déjeuner sur l'herbe*. Watercolour, 1945. In 1944 an explosion of talent occurred in Paris which seemed to represent the lightening of spirits that followed the ending of the Occupation. A group of young dancers from the Paris Opéra, led by Roland Petit and with the patronage and guidance of Christian Bérard and

Boris Kochno, emerged as the freshest of young companies, Les Ballets des Champs Elysées. Following the Diaghilev example, Petit invited the collaboration of the finest artists – a procedure he has maintained to this day – and the work of Bérard, Clavé, Cocteau, André Beaurepaire, Wakhevitch, and many more, enhanced the productions. This watercolour by Marie Laurencin is an impression of the ballet which she decorated for Petit. As with *Les Biches*, which she designed for Diaghilev in 1924, it makes entrancing use of light, clear colours and the delicious qualities of *jeunes filles en fleurs*.

150 Paul Colin, *Jean Börlin*. Poster, 1925. Colin is one of the masters of the poster, as well as being a fine stage designer, and this early example of his poster work celebrates an appearance by Jean Börlin. Börlin was principal dancer and sole choreographer of the Ballets Suédois, a company financed by the Swedish millionaire Rolf de Maré, which for five years emulated the Diaghilev ideal. Colin's poster is striking in its economy and clarity and the vitality with which the ideas of Art Deco are used.

149 Marie Laurencin, *Le Déjeuner sur l'herbe*

150 Paul Colin, *Jean Börlin*

SERGE
LIFAR

MODERN TIMES
AND
MODERN CRIMES

Ballet today exists as something on its own, quite separate from the theatre, the art-gallery and the concert hall. It has no influence on anything but itself.

Arnold L. Haskell

The vast change in styles of painting, and the diverse ways of making them in recent decades, have brought the literal, veristic representation of dancing into some disrepute. Few are the artists like Picasso or Degas who have found in ballet, or dance in any of its forms, some consistent inspiration. There has been, in past years, a nasty flurry of activity supposedly showing dancers and the dance – smudged 'impressions' of movement; deadly drawings that look as if someone has industriously copied over a photograph with tracing paper; sculpture like a haphazard agglomeration of animal concretions; smarmy delineations of dancers that copy every superficial procedure of Degas with not one iota of his anatomical understanding; portrayals of dancers, photographically exact in showing their bodies, which are akin to soft porn.

This distressing state of affairs reflects the fact that ballet itself has undergone a crisis of identity. Is it the respectable middle-brow art, found in opera houses, which beguiles its devotees with Tchaikovsky and cohorts of young women impersonating swans? Is it, rather, the portentous spectacles of Maurice Béjart for the devoted legion of the young who follow him to sports stadia and tents in search of messages about life? Or is it the truly adventurous work of American modern dancers and the uncompromising brilliance of Balanchine's New York City Ballet? Because ballet has acquired so confused an image in the public mind, it has lost its attraction for most artists and has become almost exclusively the province of the camera. The camera's effect has furthermore been to exclude the artist from any need for strict representation, and this at a time when representation itself has been so widely rejected by the most honoured and publicised artists of this century.

The result is that many literal representations of ballet are excruciatingly bad, and paintings of ballet are often at the level of chocolate box art, rehashing yet again clichés based upon Degas' paintings. Magnificent exceptions there are. We would cite the

151 Paul Colin, *Serge Lifar*. Poster, 1935. Colin's mastery of the poster is nowhere more apparent than in this large three-colour design for a recital by Lifar. It combines the bold image of Lifar's face – very stylised but utterly true – with the simplified figure of the dancer leaping in an *attitude*. The contrast between the stillness of the face and the upward movement of the body, the use of the surrounding blackness and the beautifully placed scarlet lettering, are very remarkable. See also plate 150.

152 Leslie Hurry, *Robert Helpmann*

152 Leslie Hurry, *Robert Helpmann*. Pen, ink and wash, 1942. The then Sadler's Wells (now Royal) Ballet staged Robert Helpmann's *Hamlet*, a noteworthy production, in 1942. The work was brilliantly theatrical, not least because of the superb designs by Leslie Hurry – his first work for the theatre. In 1941 Hurry had exhibited at the Redfern Gallery, showing paintings which explored an imaginative world by means of an extended Surrealist manner. Robert Helpmann visited this show and invited Hurry to decorate his forthcoming *Hamlet*. For a study of Robert Helpmann's work by Caryl Brahms (published in London in 1943) Leslie Hurry provided the dust jacket which is illustrated. It features a double portrait of Helpmann as Comus (left) and as Hamlet, in a fantasy world of ballet.

153 Bryan Organ, *Portrait of Nadia Nerina*. Oil, 1969. Bryan Organ's portrait of Nadia Nerina catches her in a pose from *The Dragonfly*. Nerina had danced this Pavlova solo with great success, and Organ fixes the essence of the movement in what seems a brilliantly immediate succession of brush strokes. The play of light through the filmy costume and its reflection on the dancer's face and breast suggest the speed of movement which is so essentially a part of this dazzling solo.

154 Marc Chagall, *Aleko : Alicia Markova as Zemphira*. Watercolour drawing, 1942. Collection of the Museum of Modern Art, New York. In 1942 American Ballet Theatre was installed in Mexico City for a five month season. During this time Leonid Massine created a ballet, inspired by Pushkin's poem *The Gypsies*, which was designed by

153 Bryan Organ, *Portrait of Nadia Nerina*

Marc Chagall. For this *Aleko* he produced decor and costumes which were a most happy marriage of his own style with the ballet's theme. The leading role of Zemphira was created for Alicia Markova, and Dame Alicia records how Chagall himself painted the heart and the tree of life on to the bodice of her costume as she wore it.

154 Marc Chagall, *Aleko*

155 Charlotte Trowbridge, *Martha Graham in 'Letter to the World'*

156 Pavel Tchelitchev, *Serge Lifar as Albrecht in 'Giselle' Act II*. Sepia pen wash on paper. Serge Lifar acquired a great reputation during the 1930s as an interpreter of the role of Albrecht in *Giselle* in his staging of that Romantic masterpiece at the Paris Opéra. Tchelitchev's superb drawing provides beautiful testimony to the power and romantic ardour of Lifar's interpretation. It is a compelling likeness, not least in the very precise rendering of Lifar's hands. Tchelitchev pinpoints the despairing energy of the hapless hero as he soars in the air – exhausted, but forced to continue dancing by the relentless Queen of the Wilis.

work of Paul Cadmus and Pavel Tchelitchev, and also the less direct contributions of distinguished painters like Berman and Bérard who were primarily involved in ballet as decorators. Because so much portrayal of dancing today never gets beyond graphic cleverness, even at its best, it is all the more rewarding to find a sculptor like William Pye intrigued by the possibilities of dance and expressive movement. In our quest for examples of contemporary painting we have found that the work of many good artists in connection with ballet has seemed peripheral – decorative, amused footnotes to the art rather than deeply concerned involvement. For the most part the contact of major artists with ballet has been in the matter of decoration: Sutherland, Piper, Ayrton, Ceri Richards in Britain; Noguchi, Johns, Rauschenberg, Stella, Warhol in America; the galaxy of artists who have worked with Roland Petit – among them Clavé, Carzou, Ernst, Delvaux; and the no less exceptional catalogue of painters who have worked for the Ballet Théâtre Contemporain in France. This activity indicates that the connection between art and ballet maintains the practical relationship initiated by Diaghilev, rather than an imaginative involvement with ballet as a source of painterly inspiration.

Paradoxically, ballet today is enjoying a popularity unknown since the heyday of the Romantic era, and is far more widespread in its manifestations. To satisfy a public demand for souvenirs of their favourite dancers and companies there are, of course, a profusion of photographs and posters. There is also a new industry in footling statuettes and drawings, but far more relevant and 'of the period' are the T-shirts and lapel buttons on sale inside and outside theatres which celebrate the names or faces of the ballet company and its stars. Taglioni appeared on soap wrappers in the 1830s; Nureyev now appears on fake dollar bills; the Soviets, Cubans and Danes put their ballerinas on postage stamps; tablets of soap are imprinted with scenes from the classical ballets.

Yet the serious involvement of artists with ballet is not impossible and not totally extinct. The camera will naturally and rightly dominate the preservation of an essentially ephemeral art. Nevertheless, the challenge to the painter remains. We can but echo David Bomberg's dictum: 'Good judgement is through good drawing . . . and when the good draughtsman draws, the muses come to dance.'

156 Pavel Tchelitchev, *Serge Lifar as Albrecht in 'Giselle'*

157 Martin Battersby, *Lynn Seymour*

157 Martin Battersby, *Lynn Seymour*. Oil, 1961. In 1961 the English *tromp-l'oeil* artist Martin Battersby held an exhibition on the theme of sphinxes; among his subjects was the young Lynn Seymour, at that time first making her mark with the Royal Ballet. Battersby saw her as a sylphide sphinx and he placed her in a nocturnal setting of a ruined abbey. The painting is a delightful caprice which also provides a touching portrait of the twenty-year-old Seymour.

158 Andy Warhol, *Merce Cunningham*. Silkscreen print. The American modern dancer Merce Cunningham has been a vastly influential figure since his first works were staged in 1952. An important aspect of his creativity has been his constant co-operation with painters in the making of his dances: Robert Rauschenberg, Jasper Johns, Frank Stella, Andy Warhol, among others, have been vitally involved in the presentation of Cunningham pieces. On some occasions this has meant that the artists have been called upon to produce aleatory settings; at other moments, the designers have left a firm imprint upon the dance from its very inception – as in the case of Rauschenberg's pointillist setting for *Summer Space*. Andy Warhol decorated *Rainforest* for

the Cunningham company, and the silver helium-filled pillows which he devised floated over the stage making their own choreographic patterns. This portrait of Cunningham is a tribute to an early dance, of 1958, in which the choreographer appeared with a chair strapped to his back. Warhol has embellished the photograph by overprinting it with a Victorian wallpaper pattern. It seems entirely in accord with Cunningham's own procedures.

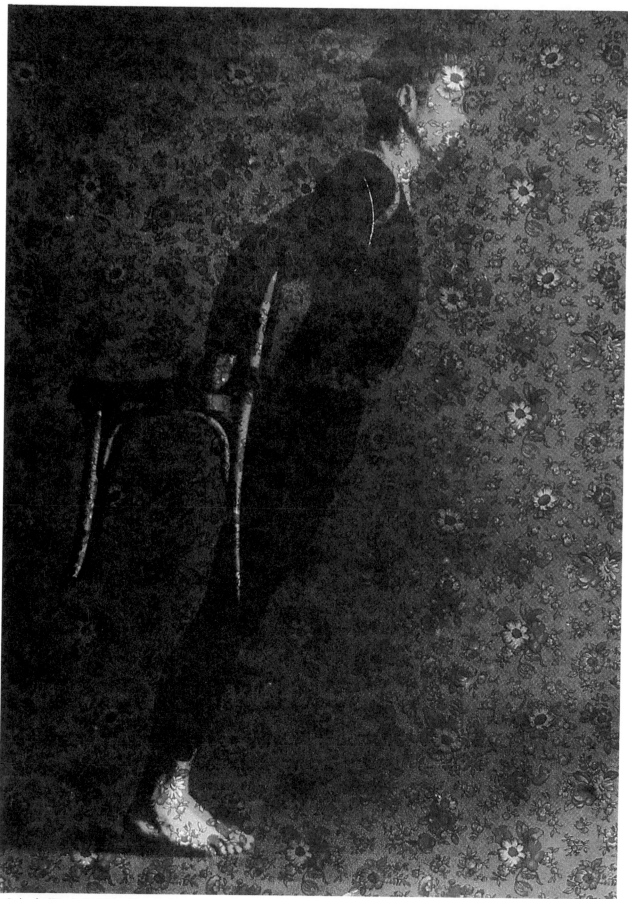

158 Andy Warhol, *Merce Cunningham*

159, 160, 161 Pavel Tchelitchev, Drawings for *Errante*. *1933. Les Ballets 1933* was a short-lived company, financed by Edward James for his wife, the dancer Tilly Losch. James's unquestioned taste as a patron of the arts guaranteed the collaboration of some of the brightest talents of the time: Balanchine, Derain, Tchelitchev, Sauguet, Milhaud, Bérard, Weill and Brecht. Among the most mysterious works created by the company was *Errante*, danced to Schubert's *Wanderer Fantasy* with choreography by Balanchine. It was designed by Tchelitchev, who gave free rein to his bizarre personal mythology and created stage pictures of ravishing beauty. The drawings illustrated are impressions of the hermaphroditic angels guiding the heroine through the fantastic action of the piece; the heroine herself is seen on the right.

159–161 Pavel Tchelitchev, Drawings for *Errante*

160

162 André Derain, *Two Dancers*

163 Joseph Cornell, *Hotel de l'Etoile*

162 André Derain, *Two Dancers*. Drawing. André Derain was first involved with the ballet when Diaghilev commissioned him to provide the decor and costumes for Massine's *La Boutique fantasque* in 1919. Thereafter he worked for many companies, always producing distinguished decoration. This drawing was used for the cover of a souvenir book of the Original Ballet Russe for a number of years from the late 1930s. The two *danseuses* in their Romantic tarlatans represent a popular public image of ballet, but Derain's clean line does not prettify them.

163 Joseph Cornell, *Hôtel de l'Etoile*. Construction. The American Surrealist Joseph Cornell was particularly fascinated by the procedures of *trompe l'oeil*, and he took this idea further by devising 'boxes' in which real objects rather than painted representations were put to surreal use. These boxes are, in effect, collages in which fragments are juxtaposed to evoke other times or other places. They are irrational, but there arise from them allusions which excite the spectator's imagination. Cornell was a balletomane and especially fond of the Romantic ballet. He used issues of *Dance Index*, the distinguished series of monographs produced in New York between 1942 and 1948, as a source for some of his imagery in such creations as *Taglioni's Jewel Casket* and his several *Homages to the Romantic Ballet*. In the *Hôtel de L'Etoile* the dancer is Lucile Grahn in *La Sylphide*.

164 Boris Chaliapin, *Alicia Markova in 'Swan Lake'*. Gouache, 1941. The super-realism of this almost life-size portrait of Alicia Markova achieves an exceptional intensity of presence. A meticulous presentation of this great English ballerina as Odette in *Swan Lake*, it catches the spiritual concentration so essentially a part of a unique performer and celebrates the enormous popularity she enjoyed in the United States.

165 Ronald Searle, Margot Fonteyn in *Hamlet*

166 Philippe Jullian, *Romantic Agony*

165 Ronald Searle, Margot Fonteyn as Ophelia in Robert Helpmann's *Hamlet*, 1943.

166 Philippe Jullian, *Romantic Agony*. Pen and ink. The author Philippe Jullian showed an equally felicitous talent as an illustrator. To both sides of his talent he brought a most perceptive eye. He seemed to take a particular delight in some of the extravagances of the ballet world and for Richard Buckle's incomparable and much lamented magazine *Ballet*, which was so influential during the six years of its existence from 1946 to 1952, Jullian contributed several sequences of funny, cruel yet truthful drawings. Shown here is the final nail in the coffin of *Giselle* – the paraphernalia of the Gothic performance style is mercilessly revealed.

167 Edward Gorey, *The Gilded Bat*. Pen and ink. The American artist and writer Edward Gorey has earned a devoted following during the past two decades through a series of books which he has written and illustrated. These combine a macabre humour with a sense of mystery and unease: the result is often disquieting, highly poetic, as well as wildly funny. Gorey is also an astute observer of the

ballet – he reportedly never misses a performance by the New York City Ballet – and his *Gilded Bat*, from which this illustration comes, is a tragi-comedy of the progress of a child, Maudie Splaytoes, who embarks upon a ballet career, changes her name to Mirella Splatover, achieves world fame and meets her doom in an aeroplane accident.

168 Saul Steinberg, *Three Dancers*. Drawing, 1951. Saul Steinberg's caricatures are far more than ephemera; they remain some of the most pertinent and valuable of social comments upon American life. This drawing made on the former premises of the School of American Ballet appeared in the American magazine *Wake*, number 10, published in New York in 1951. Steinberg indicates a great deal about the brilliant and athletic style of the dancers of the New York City Ballet.

167 Edward Gorey, *The Gilded Bat*

168 Saul Steinberg, *Three Dancers*

170 Christian Bérard, *Alice Nikitina in 'La Nuit'*

169 Feliks Topolski, *Ballerina in her Dressing Room, Monte Carlo*

169 Feliks Topolski, *Ballerina in her Dressing Room, Monte Carlo*. In 1940 the leading ballet critic Arnold Haskell arranged the publication of a book, *Ballet – to Poland*, to be sold in aid of the Polish Relief Fund. It included contributions from some of the most distinguished dance figures of the time, all of whom gave their work in aid of this excellent cause. Feliks Topolski, himself Polish, donated a portfolio of drawings of the ballet, among which was this evocative portrait of the ballerina Vera Nemchinova in her dressing room during a performance of *Coppélia*. As in the Constantin Guys drawing, plate 48, the sense of the theatre is potent.

170 Christian Bérard, *Alice Nikitina in 'La Nuit'*. Pen and watercolour, 1930. A key figure in the French art scene for twenty-five years was Christian Bérard; as painter, designer, arbiter of taste, he held a unique position. A decorator of genius, he consistently produced magic in the theatre by the simplest means, while at the same time showing an ability to create decors and costumes of the most exquisite refinement and grandest luxury. Inevitably he was attracted to the ballet, illuminating a series of works for various companies. In 1930 C. B. Cochran invited him to decorate the short ballet, *La Nuit*, which Lifar choreographed for *Cochran's 1930 Revue*.

171 Paul Cadmus, *Arabesque*. Pencil drawing, 1947. The American artist Paul Cadmus is a member of the school of painting known as Symbolic Realism, whose work was given an exhibition of exceptional interest in London in 1950. Cadmus remains one of the few artists of recent years able accurately to represent classic dancing without either vulgarity or sentimentality. His studies of dancers, nearly always in the rehearsal studio, are exact in showing how bodies work and they achieve a poetic dimension: the atmosphere, so potently created in Jerome Robbins's masterly ballet *Afternoon of a Faun*, of young bodies discovering themselves in a studio, is exactly that found in Cadmus's drawings.

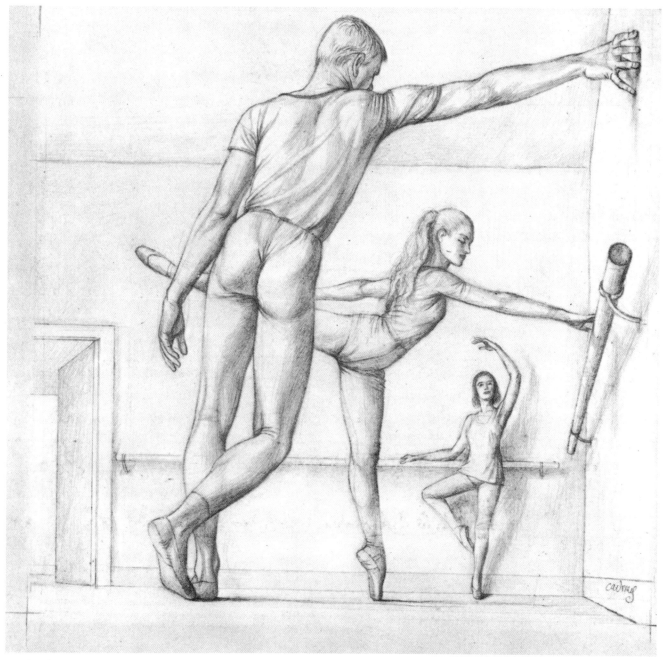

171 Paul Cadmus, *Arabesque*

172 Byrd, Poster for the Dance Theatre of Harlem. 1975. A design in electric blue and silver.

173 César, Poster for *Hopop*. 1969. Ballet Théâtre Contemporain was founded to take up residence at the Maison de la Culture in Amiens in 1968 as part of André Malraux's grand scheme for the decentralisation of the arts in France. Director of the company since its inception has been Jean-Albert Cartier, whose distinguished career as an art critic has had considerable influence upon the decorative aspects of the works staged. Cartier commissioned designs from many of the most interesting and adventurous painters and sculptors working in France. Among these was the sculptor César. His designs for *Hopop*, for which he provided the decor, reflect the Pop Art scene of the 1960s. His poster is a bold and eye-catching arrangement of colour.

174 Donn Matus, *Jewels*. Poster. Matus created three posters for the three sections of the New York City Ballet's *Jewels*, identical except for their colours – emeralds, rubies and diamonds.

172 Byrd, Poster for Dance Theatre of Harlem

173 César, Poster for *Hopop*

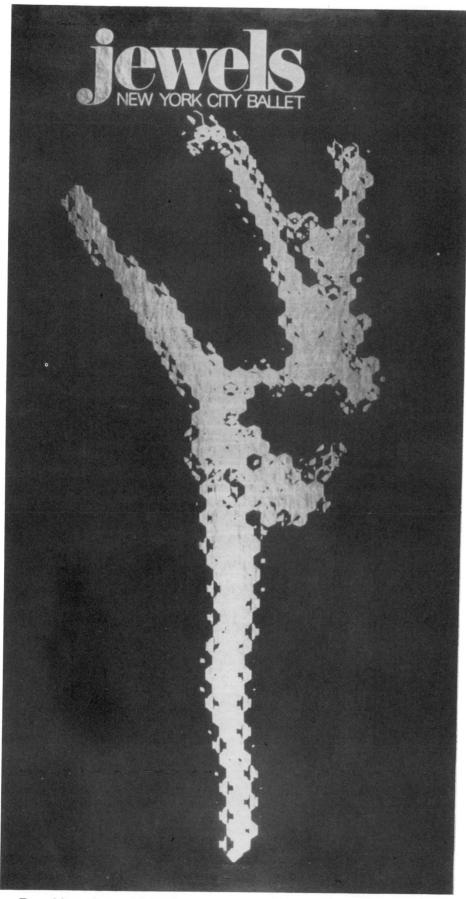

174 Donn Matus, Poster for *Jewels*

175 Enzio Frigerio, Designs for *Romeo and Juliet*

175 Ezio Frigerio, Designs for Escalus and attendants in *Romeo and Juliet*, as presented by London Festival Ballet in 1976.

176 Rex Whistler, Costume designs for *The Rake's Progress*. 1935. This ballet, by Ninette de Valois with music by Gavin Gordon, was first produced by the Sadler's Wells Ballet in 1935. Whistler's costume designs for *The Rake's Progress* were inspired by Hogarth's series of paintings.

177 Nadine Baylis, Designs for *Ziggurat*. This ballet by Glen Tetley was first produced by the Ballet Rambert in 1967. Nadine Baylis is one of the most distinguished designers working in the field of contemporary dance today.

176 Rex Whistler, Costume designs for *The Rake's Progress*

138

177 Nadine Baylis, Designs for *Ziggurat*

178, 179 Enzo Plazzotta, *Nadia Nerina*. Bronze, 1967. Among the earliest bronzes by the Italian-born sculptor Enzo Plazzotta were some studies he made in the 1960s of Nadia Nerina, then principal ballerina of the Royal Ballet. In the *Arabesque sur terre*, (179) the stretch of the body of a dancer in practice dress seems to sustain the bronze itself. Like its companion, which shows Nerina adjusting her leg warmers, this is in no sense a glamorised portrait, but an honest portrayal of a dancer at work. The hair is tied back in a bandeau; Nerina is wearing leg-warmers; the academic exactness of turn out and the anatomical logic behind it, is clearly to be seen. The bronzes also remind us of the strength and open quality of Nerina's dancing.

180 William Pye, *Nerina*. Steel sculpture, 1970. In making this standing form inspired by the dancing of Nadia Nerina, the sculptor William Pye has evoked a dancer's presence and the sense of movement inherent in a pose without sacrificing his own style. It is not a literal portrait of the dancer, but nevertheless the image of dancing, refined and transposed, is strongly present: it is rare today to find a non-representational sculptor willing and able to accept the challenge of dance.

178

178, 179 Enzo Plazzotta, *Nadia Nerina*

180 William Pye, *Nerina*

INDEX

Figures in **bold** type refer to illustrations

ACKNOWLEDGEMENTS

This book would not have been possible without the tireless help and research of Susan Hyman and Caroline Lucas. To both of them we owe an extreme debt of gratitude. We must also record our indebtedness to the generosity of Mrs Parmenia Migel Ekstrom of New York for lending so many treasures from her collection. Also in New York David Vaughan gave us valuable assistance, and we have to record our gratitude to the staff of many museums and galleries, most notably the Theatre Museum at the Victoria and Albert Museum, the Dance Collection of The Center for Performing Arts, Lincoln Center and Sotheby Parke-Bernet, New York. Christina Gascoigne kindly produced and identified gems from the Italian Renaissance theatre. To Angelo Hornak, John Webb and other photographers whose work is represented go our thanks. To Carol Venn, as always, gratitude for help in preparing the manuscript. Throughout our enterprise, Madame Maria Sackova was a constant source of inspiration.

Picture Credits
Numbers refer to plates except where marked.
Front cover: Edgar Degas, *La Danseuse au Bouquet*. Museum of Art, Rhode Island School of Design (Gift of Mrs Murray S. Danforth); Back cover: Edward Gorey, Poster for the New York City Ballet. Private collection; Page 1: Giacomo Pregliasco, *Designs for a Chinese Ballet*. Biblioteca Civica, Turin; Page 2: Eugene Berman, *Giselle*. Private collection; Page 4: John Brandard, *Carlotta Grisi in 'La Péri'*. Crown Copyright, Victoria and Albert Museum; Agence Topp, 109 (SPADEM); Bibliothèque de l'Opéra, 96 (Photo: Giraudon); Bibliothèque Nationale, 6; Birmingham Museums & Art Gallery, 63; The Brooklyn Museum (Gift of James H. Post, John T. Underwood and A. Augustus Healy), 91 (SPADEM); Bulloz, Page 7, 16, 18, 22, 100, 123 (SPADEM); Charlottenburg, 24 (Photo: Scala); Christina Gascoigne Photographs, 15; Collection Charles Gordon, 153, 179; Collection Parmenia Migel Ekstrom, Page 6, 20, 38, 55, 70, 80, 85; Crown Copyright, Victoria and Albert Museum, 1, 3, 11, 13, 26–7, 30 (Photo: Michael Holford), 36–9, 57, 60, 74 (Photo: Robert Harding), 77 (Photo: Michael Holford), 98 (Photo: Cooper-Bridgeman) (SPADEM); Dance Collection, The New York Public Library at Lincoln Center, Astor, Lenox & Tilden Foundations, 40, 68–9, 144, 158–61, 171; Fine Art Society London, 108 (Photo: Cooper-Bridgeman) (SPADEM); Frederick Gore Collection, 112 (Photo: Robert Harding); Giraudon, 134 (ADAGP), 135 (ADAGP); Glasgow Art Gallery, 92 (Photo: Cooper Bridgeman (SPADEM); Harvard Theater Collection, 64; Jeu de Paume, Paris, 99 (Photo: Scala) (SPADEM); Kunstmuseum Basel, Kupferstichkabinett, 45; Los Angeles County Museum of Art, 2; Louvre, 14 (Photo: Giraudon), 103 (Photo: Giraudon) (SPADEM); Mander & Mitchenson Theatre Collection, 67, 71, 117; Mansell Collection, 130; Mary Evans Picture Library, 10, 59, 83; Musée Bourdelle, Paris, 142 (ADAGP); Musée Carnavalet, 66 (Photo: Bulloz), 76 (Photo: Bulloz), 105 (Photo: Snark) (ADAGP); Musée des Arts Decoratifs, 75 (Photo: Bulloz); Musée d'Art Moderne, Paris, 148 (Photo: Bulloz) (SPADEM); Musée des Beaux-Arts, 133 (Photo: Giraudon) (SPADEM); Musée des Beaux-Arts, Tours, 19 (Photo: Giraudon); Musée de Toulouse-Lautrec, Albi, 93; Musées Nationaux, Paris, 29; Museum of Modern Art, New York, 120 (Gift of Edward M. M. Warburg) (ADAGP), 139 (Gift of Abbey Aldrich Rockefeller) (SPADEM), 154 (Acquired through the Lillie P. Bliss Bequest) (ADAGP); National Gallery of Art, Washington, 88 (Rosenwald Collection), 89 (Gift of Myron A. Hofer) (SPADEM), 97 (Widener Collection) (SPADEM); National Gallery of Fine Arts, Smithsonian Institution, 136 (Gift of Romaine Brooks); National Gallery of Scotland, 87 (Photo: Cooper-Bridgeman) (SPADEM), 90 (SPADEM); Nationalmuseum, Stockholm, 31; Osterreichische Nationalbibliothek, Vienna, 50; Pictor Milano, 104; Pierpont Morgan Library, 32; Private collection, 7, 9, 21, 41, 43, 47–9, 51–4, 62, 65, 72–3, 79, 81, 84, 94, 102, 110–1, 122, 124, 125–9, 132, 137–8, 140–1, 149 (ADAGP), 152, 155, 162, 164 (Photo courtesy of Boris Chaliapin), 165–9, 172–8, 180; Radio Times Hulton Picture Library, 46, 58, 101; Roger-Viollet, 61 (SPADEM), 115 (SPADEM); Royal Academy of Dancing Library, 57, 78; Snark International, 107 (SPADEM), 116 (ADAGP), 118 (SPADEM), 143 (ADAGP), 150 (ADAGP); Sotheby & Co., 86 (SPADEM), 106 (SPADEM), 119 (ADAGP), 124, 146, 151 (ADAGP); Sterling & Francine Clark Art Institute, Williamstown, Massachusetts, 95 (SPADEM); Tacoma Art Museum, Tacoma, Washington, 113 (Photo courtesy of Chapellier Galleries, Inc., New York); The Tate Gallery, London, 25, 131; Theater & Music Collection, Museum of the City of New York, 82; Trustees of the British Museum, 5, 8 (Photo: Aldus Books), 28 (Photo: John Freeman), 33 (Photo: John Freeman), 34–5, 42; Uffizi, Florence, 12 (Photo: Scala); Wadsworth Atheneum, Hartford, Connecticut, 156 (Ella Gallup Sumner and Mary Catlin Sumner Collection), 170 (Ella Gallup Sumner and Mary Catlin Sumner Collection) (SPADEM); Wallace Collection, 23 (Reproduced by permission of the Trustees); Weidenfeld & Nicolson Archives, 4, 114, 121 (SPADEM), 145 (ADAGP).